MY PATH
to
Light

How I Escaped the Darkness
of an Abusive Amish Childhood

A MEMOIR

ROSA MILLER

Ballast Books, LLC
www.ballastbooks.com

ISBN: 978-1-962202-11-4

Printed in the United States of America

Published by Ballast Books
www.ballastbooks.com

For more information, bulk orders, appearances, or speaking requests,
please email: info@ballastbooks.com

Most of the names in the book have been changed for privacy purposes.

"You can leave now."

I heard his words, but I didn't move. I was numb. My thirteen-year-old body did not understand what he had done. I hated myself for it. I hated him for it. As my senses returned from the numbness and I lay looking up at those old barn rafters, the smell of fresh-cut hay lingering in the air, I knew I couldn't continue to do life like this. I knew someone, somewhere, beyond this world, was watching over me and wanting more for me.

As he buttoned up his pants and began to move the hay for the horses, I put my clothes back on and went about my day. I noticed something different this time though. I was bleeding. All the other times, amid all the torment and anxiety of him finding me before, the result had never been blood.

What is happening? What does this mean? I can't ask Mom or Dad because they won't believe me. How could they? That would make them choose between me, the fourth-born daughter, or their first-born son.

Those were the questions I was grappling with at the time. I was not special in any way, so why would they believe me over him? And was this the only value I had to offer—serving others in any way possible, even if it destroyed me in the process?

I had no idea that these questions would continue to plague me for a long time to come—just as Wilbur would continue to abuse me, his own little sister.

Contents

Foreword

*I*t's a bright September morning. The door to my deck is propped open to the Mandeville vine, grown far beyond the top point of its trellis, smothered in dozens of large pink trumpet blossoms. Beyond the flower-covered deck, I have a full view of the grassy peninsula curving its way into the large pond behind our home. Past the pond to the west, the marsh stretches for miles before it reaches the lake. To the east are the Rocky Mountains. A breeze brings the smell of newly cut grass and the sound of the geese squawking as they gracefully slide into the sparkling water. Everything I see, hear, smell, and even taste brings me hope, joy, and light—so much light. A high-frequency weaving of light through every part of my world. Knowing that winter is just weeks away, at this moment, I soak in the fresh air, warm sunshine, and life-affirming reality of Mother Earth. Today, this gift of beauty perfectly embodies *My Path to Light*.

It's not easy to read about stolen innocence, the suffering of a child, a stalwart family's demonic secrets, or a community of faith gone blind. But still, I read, compelled by a child's strength, vision, and determination. This story is complete in the most remarkable sense because, even in her solitary agony, here is a girl who somehow maintained her connection to goodness and faith and clung to the knowledge that she is loved, seen, heard, and even held by heaven. *My Path to Light* is a most authentic hero's journey.

As you read, you will likely feel what I have felt: anger, dismay, disgust, and even a moment of questioning the goodness of a God who would allow any child to be treated with such evil disregard. Yet Rosa holds the truth in her core and bravely brings light to her experiences. In the pages of her memoir, she seems to maneuver through the dark night, characterized by maddening paradoxes and puzzling contradictions, without losing hope, without turning against the God of her family tradition. Rather, in the most authentic sense, Rosa uses the misconceptions, lies, shunning, and darkness of unrighteous dominion as a holy tool to distinguish the light. To learn to discern. To choose freedom over fear. Her transcendence out of the hell of religious and sexual abuse is something truly profound and inspiring, a powerful guide for any wounded soul. And, I believe, Rosa is precisely the teacher each of us needs as we discover our own path to wholeness.

Like each of us, Rosa intuitively knows the truth, and her choice to keep believing in a Creator who loves perfectly despite the misuse of "holy authority" against the vulnerable ultimately liberated her. This can be a holy guide to freedom for anyone with ears to hear or eyes to see into the heart of hope.

—Rachelle Pace Castor,
advocate for those seeking to shed
their abusive environments and grow
beyond the boundaries set around them

CHAPTER ONE

Amish Life

*T*here were only a few things I truly cared about growing up, but one thing I consistently desired from age five was to be a good and godly person. Sometimes, however, I wondered whether being a good and godly person was even possible.

I grew up in a large Amish community in the middle of Iowa. To give you a bit of context, Amish was more than a culture to me for the first nineteen years of my life. It was a religion that I was taught and practiced from the cradle. One fundamental part of that religion is this: if you want to go to heaven, you have to continue in the faith you were born into. For me, that meant being Amish—forever.

You know how the Western Christian churches of today all have Christ as the savior in common but also have unique doctrines to the individual church? The same applies to the Amish communities. While there are a few baseline similarities across all the Old Order Amish, each community you walk into has something unique to them.

My personal experience is also special to me. For many years, my journey was tightly knit into the Amish religion. To be clear, I am not trying to disparage or discount the Amish religion by sharing my opinions and experiences. This story is not about any religion's rights or wrongs but how I found redemption, grace, and forgiveness despite the odds against me from the time I was a young child despite having been raised in a religion that has strong values and encourages a simple lifestyle.

One famous saying among the Amish churches is, "Where there are no rules, there is no ordnung." Basically, that means if there are no rules on everything, community members will not know right and wrong. Therefore, the elders have to make rules and enforce them. As a result, each community has regulations defining rights and wrongs for its members.

Typically, Amish rules are formed based on the ideas and beliefs of the community-founding leaders. However, shunning and adult baptism are two things held among all Amish communities.

Shunning is a form of separation that happens to a church member who has sinned. In essence, this person would be parted from the rest of the church members. The baún is the severest type of shunning in this culture. In the community I grew up in, one way this shunning was enforced was through eating. The sinner could not serve themselves from the same pots of food or sit at the same table as other members of the church. A person who was not being shunned could prepare the sinner's plate, and they could have the same food as long as they—the sinner—had not physically taken any food out of the pot themself. In general, shunning continues until the separated member comes before the church, confesses their sin, and asks for forgiveness from the rest of the congregation.

Adult baptism usually occurs once an individual is between the ages of sixteen and twenty-one. Before baptism, there are six classes over twelve weeks through the summer to learn the church's rules, beliefs, and expectations. I was age seventeen when I went through this same ritual.

Aside from shunning and adult baptism, there are other elements of Amish culture that are fairly consistent, though the details may vary from community to community. For example, the Amish have a dress code for both men and women. Family or community members sew the clothes themselves because of the specific regulations. This allows the styles to align with each community's standards. I never had any store-bought clothes except for the basic undergarments.

One aspect of the dress code for women includes the head covering. In our community the sloppier the head covering, the more godly or less worldly one was considered. If my head covering was too neat, we would receive complaints from the church officials, and because I wasn't baptized yet, Mom and Dad bore the brunt of the punishment from the church. My punishment from Mom was that she would iron or fix my head covering after I had ironed it to make it as sloppy as possible in hopes of getting less complaints.

Church services are on a rotating basis. Each family in the community takes their turn. If it is a large enough community—at least sixty to seventy families—the community is divided into congregations, allowing church services to be in a family's home or a large shed. These religious gatherings occur every other Sunday to give the ministers and people a break or chance to attend another congregation's service in the community.

Growing up in my community, church services were usually three hours long. They began at 9 a.m. and ended around 12:00 p.m. to 12:30 p.m., depending on the promptness of the speaking preacher. However, if there were problems or concerns, the church members would have to stay longer after the preaching to address them. The little ones and non-members would be dismissed so only members would hear about and vote on how to handle these issues.

If a member had committed an offense or misbehaved during the previous two weeks, this was the time for them to confess. Afterward, the church members would vote on whether or not they wanted the baún lifted or forgiven that day. However, the church could not punish a person until they became baptized. If an unbaptized child was misbehaving or causing too much trouble in the community, the church would instead punish the parents to try to get things back to how they thought they should be.

In the Amish community, there is no electricity in the homes. Accordingly, during my childhood, we could not have phones. If we needed to make a call, we had to use the English (as the Amish call the non-Amish) neighbor's phone or a phone shack, one of which was on the edge of an English neighbor's property with a phone line hooked up in the shed.

To give further insight into Amish culture, day-to-day transportation is horse drawn. Occasionally, the Amish hire a taxi to go places, like in the case of an emergency, a funeral, a wedding, or to visit family in another community. Other than that, we relied on buggies pulled by horses to get from one place to another.

At the age of seventeen, a person is considered a youngie, meaning they can begin participating in youth group activities, meeting Sunday nights for a singing group, dating, and partying, depending on what community they live in. Youngie decide when they want to be baptized into the church.

In the first Amish community we lived in, the youth were big into the party lifestyle. This is the stage of a person's life when they get to exercise their rebellion or wild side against the Amish religion by partying the weekend away with other youngie while remaining in good standing with the Amish church. There is one condition: the person has to be unbaptized. Otherwise, it can cause problems. Becoming baptized shows the community that one is ready to put away the partying lifestyle, commit to the church rules, and prepare for marriage, so after baptism, the youngie wild stage is officially over.

Growing up Amish sometimes means moving around frequently. If there are too many instances of rule-breaking, then a family can and often does move to another community where the rules differ. Sometimes, a family can become targeted, and when this happens, they end up having more problems with the church. What causes a family to be targeted? It can be as simple as the adults not agreeing on the same principles. If one family doesn't like another family because of some unresolved offense that happened between them—especially if the offended party happens to be in good standing with the leaders and they want to cause problems for the other family—they will essentially be a tattletale for the church. At this point, the targeted family often seeks another community to start fresh in.

Although the Amish have very specific laws concerning most things you can see and touch, there are some communities that have very few laws emphasizing the importance of good morals and honesty. Nobody would say that those virtues aren't important; the idea is that they are just a given and everyone should know to uphold them. Therefore, there is theoretically no need to make a law concerning them. However, a key phrase in Amish culture is "where there are no laws, we will not know right from wrong." So it seems logical to me, that Amish laws should address morality and integrity.

All in all, Amish lifestyle has many elements that are consistent from one community to the next and many more that vary. Hopefully, this crash course on the foundations of Amish culture will prepare you for what's to come—my story of finding the path to light through the darkness.

CHAPTER TWO

A Prized Doll

*T*hroughout my childhood, I always felt like I didn't belong—like I was a misfit—but I knew I had to find a way to live the Amish lifestyle because practicing anything else meant I was going to hell. At least, that's what was instilled in me from a young age.

My family consisted of fifteen children—eleven girls and four boys. I had two older brothers and three older sisters, which made me number six from the top down. Being part of a large family meant life was always busy with lots happening. One could always find a buddy to play with. I never had to be alone if I did not want to be. There was always some work to do, so playing quietly and out of sight of my older siblings and parents was vital as I grew older. It started out with me wanting to slip out of as many chores as possible, but with time, it became a survival tactic. My parents were so busy trying to make a living for the large family and please the elders or other people of the community that their children often only got attention from them if they had caused problems. No, this isn't necessarily the case for every child in every Amish family, but it was my experience. I got to the point that I didn't want to see my parents other than in passing for fear I had done something wrong. In many ways, I associated them with chastisement.

I *hated* confrontation, so I learned to fly under the radar. The more invisible I was, the better it was for me. This meant I caused no problems with any of my siblings. I agreed with them quickly and never complained. Having fifteen children to care for, feed, clothe, and keep healthy did not leave much time for my parents to foster good relationships with each child. As a result, I always felt like my feelings didn't matter, and looking back, I can see that it started with my beloved doll.

Amish families are large and spread apart. It was a rare treat to have a family visit overnight. I remember one such occasion happening when I was five. Two of my aunts and their families came to our community to spend some time with us. Two aunts with their families also already lived in my community, so we had to share our company. One day during this visit, we hosted three of my aunts and their families at our house. I was super excited to have lots of cousins coming. It also meant hard work for Mom and my older sisters, but I was too little to understand. I was just looking forward to having quality time with my cousins.

Finally, they arrived, and we decided to play with dolls. There were eight of us little girls who wanted to play. Most of our dolls were nothing fancy. They had no detailed faces or hair for definition, but we were happy with them.

However, I had gotten a doll as a Christmas present from school that year, and it was beautiful. The face had some definition, and the doll was made with a unique washable material. It even had a complete set of clothes: a dress and apron, a head covering (cöeply), a bonnet, a shawl, and booties. It was the best thing I had ever owned, so naturally, I was very protective of my doll.

The first step in setting up our baby play was to choose our families. We'd place all our dolls and younger siblings who wanted to play in a circle and then take turns choosing our playing families. However, my doll was *not* up for picking! I was excited to show them my prized possession, but I wasn't planning to have it put into the choosing ring. In my mind, it was a given that I should be able to have it as my baby. After all, we had plenty of other dolls, and I was more than willing to share them. Together, we decided the four older girls (five- to seven-year-olds) would be moms, and the rest would be our children.

As we got started with our game, I clutched my doll, intent on having her as my baby. But one of my out-of-state visiting cousins wanted my doll too. The argument got heated, and two of the older in-state cousins got involved. Still, I was adamant about not giving up my prize. I could not understand why I should have to give my doll to my cousin to play with just because she wanted it. She could use one of the other dolls. Did what I want not matter?

When my cousins could not persuade me to give up my doll, they told me I was wicked and that God would make me burn in hell for my selfishness. An innocent little girl, I did not know what hell was, so I asked them to explain it. I wanted to see if it would be worth giving up my doll. In response, my cousins vividly described hell as a hot, blazing fire that burns forever and ever and never ends. In an ominous tone, they warned that would be my fate for all eternity if I was too selfish to give up my doll. My seven-year-old cousin, in particular, was sure I'd be condemned to hell if I chose not to share.

Some parental supervision would have been excellent at that point; however, we never went to our parents for help with such trivial matters, and this time was no different. We just fought amongst ourselves and figured it out the best we could.

Every week in our washhouse, we lit a fire under the water kettle to heat our laundry and bathing water. So I knew what a hot, blazing fire looked like. As a five-year-old, I was terrified to imagine that God would ever confine me in such a place simply for not giving up my doll. Unsurprisingly, I decided my treasured toy was not worth going to hell for and reluctantly allowed my cousin to use it. After I repented for my selfish ways, the rest of our playtime was uneventful. However, I could not erase the image of me burning in the fire. That mental picture haunted me for many years to come.

After the doll incident, I could no longer stand up for myself in *anything* for fear that I would burn in hell. I had learned that if I always gave others what they wanted from me, God would spare me from the burning fire.

As a result of this experience, I began having nightmares about hell and became a very fearful little girl. If I could think of something frightening, I was afraid and then dreamed about it happening to me. For example, we raised fryers to butcher and sell, so we frequently had English people coming to our home to either pick up or place orders. If I happened to be out in the yard when someone came up our driveway, I would immediately fear I was going to be kidnapped and taken from my home. Eventually, we could no longer visit anywhere without me coming home crying inconsolably. Irrationally, I was convinced I had done something terrible that would get me put into the burning fire.

When I had my crying spells, Dad was always the one who tried to comfort me. I don't remember telling him where my overwhelming fear came from; in fact, I didn't realize where it originated myself until years later. But my dad did attempt to soothe me when I was overcome by this crippling anxiety.

Eventually, I opened up to Dad about my worries and said I didn't want to go to hell. In turn, he tried to reassure me that I would not go to hell if I was a good girl and obeyed my parents. So I took comfort in following the rules. If I was told these were the rules to be good, I did them. I became excellent at observing the laws of our family, both the spoken and unspoken.

One of the unspoken rules was to share and give others what they wanted from me, no matter the circumstances. I learned it was okay for me to go without as long as I helped another person have what they wanted. This would ultimately influence my response to the trauma I was soon to endure as just a little girl.

CHAPTER THREE

A Taste of Evil

*I*t was a beautiful evening on the farm. I was seven years old. Because it was summer, I only had a few chores. My oldest brother, Wilbur, who was thirteen, was completing his own tasks while my two younger sisters and I played contentedly in the barn.

I loved being around the horses, so after some time, I left my sisters and went to help Wilbur feed them. Halfway through, Wilbur abruptly stated he wanted to take a break and hold me. I thought this was strange as my brother had never tried to hold me any other time. We weren't done feeding the animals, and it would soon be time to bring in the cows to begin the milking process. But he insisted, sitting down on a five-gallon bucket with an expectant look. I decided why not, knowing I shouldn't deny anyone something I could give them. Innocent as ever, I allowed him to hold me.

To my immense horror, Wilbur promptly put his hand under my dress and tried to touch my vagina. Immediately, I wanted off his lap! It no longer mattered that I would deny him something he wanted. Instinctively, I knew what Wilbur was doing was wrong, but he wouldn't let me go. He told me he wanted to touch me and that it would be fun. It sure did not feel like fun to me! I attempted to lurch away, intent on escaping his seeking hands, but he kept a firm grip and continued trying to touch me.

I was desperate to get away when, unaware of the situation, one of my older sisters, Magdalena, walked into the barn to begin the milking. As soon as she arrived, Wilbur told me he would let me go if I promised to come to his room once he was in bed. At that point, I would have told him anything just to be released, so I quickly agreed to meet him. He finally let me go with a firm reminder to come to him later that night.

That evening after supper, when Wilbur was getting ready for bed, he came to me and, in a whisper, reminded me of my promise. However, I refused to go with him. I didn't know what was in store for me, but I did know that what had happened earlier was not something I wanted any part in. Typically, I would try to hide after supper so I wouldn't have to help with drying the dishes, but that night, I was more than happy to stay in plain sight and help out.

After a failed attempt to make me keep my promise, Wilbur retreated upstairs to his room. I breathed a quiet sigh of relief, thinking I was safe. However, after a few minutes, Wilbur called down, asking me to bring him water. When I didn't fall for this trick, he yelled at Mom and pleaded for her to have me bring him a glass of water. I told Mom I was busy, insisting Wilbur could come downstairs and get his own drink. Mom must have agreed because she asked him to do it himself, to which he replied, "I can't; I'm undressed. Have Rosanna bring it up to me." At this point, Mom told me, "Just behave yourself and take him some water. It won't take you that long. You can finish drying dishes when you come back."

Realizing I would have to complete this dreaded task, my mind started working overtime, trying to find a solution before I got to my destination. My brothers, Wilbur and Patrick, shared a room that was also the hallway. Our stairway had a half wall instead of a full wall, which we called a banister. As I came up the stairs, I decided I would set the water on the banister and hightail it out of there. However, given all my resistance leading up to this, Wilbur was ready for any tricks. When I got to the top of the stairs, there he was! As soon as I set the glass down, he grabbed my arm. After a battle of wills and strength, he took me to his bed and touched and rubbed my vagina until he was satisfied. Then, he finally allowed me to leave.

After he released me, I returned downstairs in a daze only to find that the dishes had been completed while I was gone. I felt so filthy! Why would something like that happen? Why did it happen to me? Had I done something wrong, and was this God's way of punishing me? I felt like my life had just been shattered, and the rest of my family didn't even know anything had happened. I was both glad and sad that no one else was aware of it—glad because it helped me hide my shame from others and sad because no one was there to help me.

My thoughts were all over the place. *Why would Wilbur do something like that to me? What did I do to deserve that kind of treatment? And why had my mother not tried to save me? I know what happened was wrong, but Wilbur said it was fun. How could that be?*

After this, I figured I was on my own, as I could not comprehend why my mom would have sent me into such an environment. Looking back, that is the night I lost my mom emotionally.

A few months later, my younger siblings and I were playing hide and seek. Dusk was just settling outside, and we had a gas light in the kitchen area but no light in the living room—perfect for hide and seek. There was a mattress on the floor in the living room area, and us little ones were having a lot of fun with our game when Wilbur entered and lay down on the mattress.

I thought nothing of it as we continued playing. I figured I would be safe with others in the room with me. However, at one point, when we were running to hide, I passed too close by the mattress. Wilbur grabbed me, pulled me under him, and proceeded to fondle me again. When I fought him, he pinned me down with his body and started rubbing his dick on my vagina.

My little sisters asked me why I wasn't playing anymore, and Wilbur told them, "Keep playing your game. Rosanna will come help again soon." So they continued running around, completely oblivious to the horror I was enduring. I was so humiliated. How could it get any worse than that? Here I was being fondled by my oldest brother right in the middle of our home with my little siblings watching, and there was nothing I could do about it. I was too ashamed to cry out for help, thinking I deserved that kind of treatment if my brother was giving it to me. The tears streaming down my face didn't matter; no one could see them anyway, as there was not enough light in the room.

After this incident, I realized that I truly wasn't safe in my home. No matter who was around, Wilbur would find a way to separate me, and it clearly didn't matter if my younger siblings saw him either.

That night perpetuated a nightmarish reality from which I could not escape. I'm thankful I didn't know how long I would live in that hell. The fear of being hunted and caught to be used as my captor desired and for as long as he desired overwhelmed me. My spirit was crushed from the weight of this nightmare, and I was slowly being destroyed from the inside out. Sometimes, I wished Wilbur would just kill me. However, as my will to live freely grew, I began watching over my shoulder, expecting Wilbur in the most unexpected places.

The freedom of the farm I loved had become a trap, a fever dream of the worst kind. I no longer wanted to do anything alone. I developed a sixth sense and could always tell when my brother was around. On many occasions, this helped me evade his clutches. I had planned escape routes for every building on the farm, and these also proved helpful—until Wilbur realized I had them, and he became craftier too.

To my utter dismay, I soon realized I wasn't the only one my brother was molesting when one of my younger sisters commented that she hated what Wilbur did to her. At first, I was wary and cautiously asked her about it. She proceeded to tell me in detail how he touched her. I was horrified and felt totally helpless! How could I protect her? I didn't think I could depend on Mom to help me, as she had not stopped Wilbur from hurting me. To be fair, I had not told my mother about Wilbur, but as a seven-year-old, I thought my mom knew everything.

I felt responsible for looking out for my sisters' safety. From that moment forward, if I knew Wilbur would be alone with one of my younger sisters, I would tag along with them. Sometimes, Wilbur refused to allow more than one of us girls to help him, so I would offer myself in their place, taking the pain so my sisters wouldn't have to. I could not let my sisters be hurt if there was something I could do to prevent it. I hated it, and I came to hate my brother. To me, Wilbur was a monster! But Wilbur was also my brother. How could he be both a monster and my brother?

CHAPTER FOUR

Trash Everywhere

I woke to a steady *wrr, wrr, wrr*. At first, I was a little disoriented. Where was I? Then, it all came back to me: I was in the van that was taking my mom, my sisters, and a few close friends to our new home eighty miles away, close to the Minnesota border. Everything was quiet, as most of the people in the van were sleeping. As we neared our destination, one by one, everyone woke up. It was my first time seeing where we were moving to. I was interested in what my new surroundings would be like.

About a quarter mile from our driveway, there were two big hills. The taxi driver was someone my parents knew, and he decided to have some fun with us. We started down the first hill, and as we got close to the bottom, the driver accelerated before starting straight up the next one. There was a collective "oh" from his passengers. I felt like I had left my stomach behind. As the driver started laughing at our reactions, we realized he had deliberately driven in that manner to get a response. We all laughed too, which helped alleviate the tension building in the vehicle as we neared our new home.

My older sisters, Bertha and Larissa, were unhappy to be making a move. Not only were they being forced to leave their friends behind—as we all were—but they were also both old enough to participate in youth activities and start dating. Bertha had a boyfriend and Larissa was interested in a boy in the community we were leaving behind. So, as you can imagine, they weren't too eager about this next Chapter for our family.

My folks did not like the weekend partying lifestyle that was typical for the youngie in our old community, so we were relocating to another community where those activities were not accepted. This community had stricter rules and higher expectations for their youngie.

We slowed down as we approached our driveway, which consisted of a quarter-mile-long dirt path. It was early spring, and with the frost leaving the ground, the driveway became a muddy, slippery mess. We drove up the path between two fields lined with trash piles everywhere. After rounding an S curve, we caught our first glimpse of the house. There was trash and tall weeds as far as we could see. The weeds were taller than the fence in front of the house! I did not understand the church and its rules then, but I saw our place's mess and began to have my own misgivings about the move.

The moving van had arrived before us and was backed up as close to the house as possible. We had a couple of livestock trailers, a flatbed semi-trailer with farm and shop equipment, and the semi van with household stuff that needed unloading that day. Dad and my two older brothers split up and rode with different drivers. There were horses and buggies there too, as some of the people from the community had come to help us unload our belongings from the various trailers.

When we arrived, I followed Mom into our new home. We had a nice big kitchen and living room that Dad and some of his friends had remodeled a few weeks previously. We turned what had been the living room into a bedroom for Mom and Dad on the main level, and then we had three more bedrooms on the second floor. The south bedroom was large, and there were two smaller ones off to the north. Bertha got the middle bedroom, and my two older brothers shared the far north one. Dad put a partition in the bigger south bedroom to make a small one for Larissa. Elsie, who was the youngest girl then, slept in there too. The other four girls and one younger brother shared the other half of what had been the bigger bedroom.

Some of the womenfolk arrived mid-morning bearing lunch. They had cooked a hot meal at their homes and brought it over to share with everyone. This was a big help to Mom, as she didn't have her stove set up yet.

All in all, that day went by fast. With all the community helpers, unloading the household trailer took little time. The guys hauled in the furniture and boxes while Mom indicated where to place things. The womenfolk who had brought lunch helped with the unpacking too.

Setting up the kitchen and living room stoves was the priority. Dad and a few other menfolk took charge of that while the rest continued to haul furniture and boxes. Meanwhile, the womenfolk went to work setting up and preparing the beds as others unboxed the kitchen supplies. After the men had unpacked the household items, they went outside to unload the shop and farm equipment. We had one large cement bunker where the outdoor equipment was placed. The livestock was taken care of as it arrived throughout the day too. Luckily, before our big moving day, Dad had brought hay and such to our new place so that some necessary animal supplies would be waiting for when the animals arrived.

I had not seen my older brothers and sisters all day. My brothers had been outside working with livestock, and my sisters had stayed in the van most of the day with their friends who had traveled with us that morning. When it was time for everyone to go home that night, it was a battle for my parents to keep their older children from leaving with the drivers. It was a hard move for Bertha in particular. She was leaving behind all her youth friends and new boyfriend.

After chores and supper, as us younger girls were preparing for bed, the reality of our move hit me. I would no longer see my cousins or the friends I had made in school regularly. After the lights were out, I lay on my bed and cried.

There were piles of trash outside every window of our new house. There was trash in the area that would be our yard, behind the barn, and in the fields. Plus, old, broken-down buildings littered the farmyard. For the next two years, we stayed busy cleaning up the place. While we children went to school, my older siblings and dad stayed home and cleaned one trash pile at a time. I remember coming home from school each day and looking around to see what section of garbage had been taken care of that day. I was happy not to have to do all the trash removal, but adjusting to a new school was not the easiest thing either.

One of the main attractions school had for me was that I would be away from Wilbur. I could relax my guard a little during the day. However, in the afternoons when we got home from school, the first thing I wanted to know was *where is Wilbur?*

The school we were attending had an Amish male teacher. The rules and practices were utterly different. It was a one-room classroom with first through eighth grades attending. Every morning, we began our day with two songs. Each day, the students—two daily—took turns picking and leading those songs. On Friday, we had to sing German tunes. The lineup went from oldest to youngest, but the first graders were exempt from song leading until they were able to read.

Patrick, my older brother, was one of the older students, so his turn to lead singing came very quickly after we started attending school. When it was his first time to lead the song, we sat for a good ten minutes waiting for him to make a selection. When the teacher eventually realized that he was not planning to make a choice anytime soon, the teacher did it instead, and we continued with our morning routine. I do not know what consequences Patrick faced for pulling a stunt like that, but the next time it was his turn to choose the song, we didn't have to wait very long for him to begin. His lead singing wasn't perfect, but with time and a little bit of "try," he improved.

We got three recesses—fifteen minutes in the morning and afternoon and a half-hour break for lunch. Our subjects were different too. We had spelling, reading, penmanship, arithmetic, and English as our main subjects, with geography and history alternating every other year.

With time, I made friends with the girls in my class. I felt lucky that there were only girls—no boys. Because of the interactions with my brother, I had learned to place all boys in the unsafe category, so I was happy that none were in my grade at this school. After the first year, though, another school in our community had a fire, and instead of building another schoolhouse right away, half of those families joined our classroom the following fall. It was a big enough schoolhouse, and with some remodeling, it worked great for more students.

Now that more girls were in our school, I became friends with some of them as well. Though I was friendly with many other girls, I had one best friend: Martha. She was two months younger than me but taught me many things. Martha had a better relationship with her older sister Elnora than I had with any of my older sisters, and she taught me what Elnora taught her. I felt very fortunate to have a friend like her.

CHAPTER FIVE

Life on the Farm

*W*e had settled into a routine, and life in our home was not as bad as I had first thought it might be. Helping Dad and the boys with outside work was a common occurrence for the girls. Although I was too young to assist with the heavier labor, I could drive the horses when needed.

One day, Dad and Wilbur were doing some work with the horses in one of the outbuildings close to the garden area while Mom and some of us girls were working in the garden. I was young enough that I floated between the two groups. When the menfolk were done with the horses, Wilbur was supposed to take them back to the barn, but instead of doing it himself, he asked me to do it.

Instantly, I became suspicious. I didn't trust him, so I took off running, headed for the garden area. However, much to my consternation, Wilbur had Dad call me back to take the horses to the barn "like a big helper." Knowing I had to move quickly, I waited until Wilbur was busy helping Dad with something. Then, I hurriedly took the team of horses to the barn and put them in their stalls without tying them up. To my relief, I was out of the barn again before Wilbur could enter.

As I was heading out the side door, Wilbur was coming toward the barn. When he asked me if I had tied up the horses, I said, "No, they will be fine." Brows knitting together, Wilbur instructed me to go back and tie them up, but I refused. He knew I had no intention of entering that barn with him in the vicinity, so instead of dealing with the horses himself, Wilbur called out, "Dad! Rosanna didn't tie up the horses! Make her go back and tie them up."

I quickly responded, "Wilbur can do it himself if he wants them tied up. He is going to the barn anyway."

"Dad, I can't," Wilbur protested. "I have other things I need to do. Have Rosanna do it."

At that point, Dad insisted that I help out. Hope of reprieve extinguished, I gritted my teeth, realizing I had no choice but to follow orders. Dread building with each footstep, I went back to the barn to tie up the horses. I was totally outraged, especially since Wilbur was right beside me the whole time, waiting for me to complete the task that he couldn't complete because he had "other things to do." After a struggle, Wilbur took me to the hayloft and used me to his liking. It was becoming a routine that I hated more and more.

Gardening was a huge part of keeping us busy in the early spring and summer. Then, there was harvesting and canning in the fall. These were girls' work in our family, along with laundry, cooking, cleaning, yard work, mowing, and weeding the garden. In our family, the boys often didn't have to help with girls' work. They would have had opportunities to assist but were excused from it because they had other harder, more demanding jobs to do. But on the flip side, we girls often ended up helping accomplish the boys' "harder" chores as the girls outnumbered the boys in our family by a long shot.

Each day, we spent long hours out in the field with the horses and farm equipment just in preparation. Then, the planting took place. Once the crops began to grow, the corn had to be cultivated; otherwise, after a certain point, it would be too tall to cultivate. After that, we were done with the corn until it was ready to be husked in the fall.

We also had oats and hay. Once planted, the oats didn't need a lot of extra work until they were ready to be cut. However, we had hay in stages throughout the summer and typically at least three different cuttings per field.

Haying was a big project that could take a few days to complete once the cutting and racking were done. After the hay was cut, Dad let it dry in the field before we loaded it in a wagon and brought it to the barn, where we had the baler set up. Once it was baled, we would send the hay up into the hayloft with an elevator. There, we had at least two people ready to stack the bales.

Dad would check the weather report in the newspaper whenever we were preparing to start another haying session.

Sometimes, we had to bale our hay when it was still pretty green, which meant it didn't dry well in the field, if there was rain in the forecast. When that happened, we had to salt the hay bales on each level as we stacked them in the barn so the hay wouldn't overheat as it dried over the summer. We didn't want to cause a fire!

When I was eight, I started to fill the role of driver during haying season. That meant I would drive one team of horses during the hay-loading process and then transport a load of hay from the field up to the barn where Dad was waiting to bale it. Typically, Wilbur would do the loading, Dad would do the baling, and two older sisters would take care of the stacking. Meanwhile, Patrick was driving the second team of horses. As the children grew, the jobs shifted, and I ended up in the hayloft with Patrick stacking once my younger sisters were old enough to take over the driving.

I loved the outside and the hard physical work, as it helped me grow stronger, and I had hopes that one day I would be strong enough to physically protect myself from Wilbur. At the same time, I was always watching over my shoulder, afraid to be caught unawares by my brother.

When the oat-cutting season arrived, Dad or one of my older siblings would cut the oats during the day. In the evening, after the milking, anyone in the family who was big enough to handle a shaft of oats was out in the field, shocking oats until dark. This involved making small houses with seven sheathes or bundles of oats. We used six bundles to create the base and one for the top. When done correctly, the top one protected the bundles underneath from the rain. This was to get the oats off the ground and help with drying.

Sometimes, we had other families in the neighborhood come to help. When that happened, we also went to their house and helped with their shocking. Our closest Amish neighbors were three miles away. It wasn't all that far, but it felt like a long way when traveling by horse and buggy.

Once the shocking was complete and the oats were dried, the thrashing began. This was usually a community event where the whole neighborhood (or at least the families that had oats) would help each other. This was one instance when only the boys and men did the work. The women had their own jobs cut out, cooking for the thrashing crew.

After the morning mess was cleared, the noon meal prep began. When the thrashing crew was at our house, it meant cooking a large meal for lunch and preparing a snack for around 3:30 p.m. to 4:00 p.m. The meal usually consisted of meat, potatoes, bread, vegetables, and a salad for the main course. Then, there were pies, cake, and puddings for dessert. After the men had gotten their fill, we womenfolk ate and cleaned up. It was usually a big mess and one of my least favorite jobs.

After that, we would begin the afternoon snack prep. We usually had meat sandwiches and homemade ice cream. The bread for the sandwiches was always baked the day before, and the meat was stored in the basement, making the sandwich prep easy. The ice cream was more time-consuming. We used a five-quart hand-cranked ice cream bucket to make the frozen dessert and then utilized our ice from the icehouse for the freezing. All in all, the cranking/freezing process took about fifteen to twenty minutes. When the afternoon snack was ready, we would take it out to the front yard and set it up under the biggest tree where the thrashers could easily access the snacks while waiting in the shade for their turn to unload their oats or before heading back into the field for another load.

One winter evening, my siblings, Dad, and I were in the barn starting chores. We had no electricity, so we used gasoline lanterns for light. However, we didn't take the lanterns into the hayloft because of the fire hazards. It had gotten dark before the hay was thrown down from the hayloft, so Wilbur wanted me to help him by holding the flashlight while he completed that task. Knowing what was in store, I ducked behind the ally divider, but Wilbur knew where I was and told Dad I was hiding instead of helping him. In an impatient tone, Dad told me to stop being contrary and hold the flashlight for Wilbur.

In desperation, I tried to get one of my sisters to come with me, but Wilbur wouldn't allow it on the basis we would play instead of paying attention and directing the light where he needed it. Not knowing what I knew, Dad got frustrated and told me to behave myself and shine the flashlight so we could get on with our other chores.

At that moment, all the faith I had in my dad went down the drain. This only reinforced the fact that I no longer felt safe anywhere, even among my family. I realized Wilbur would find ways to get me alone, even if that meant getting me in trouble with my parents.

As the days turned into years, I found myself increasingly determined to find a way to avoid being consumed by fear and resentment for my brother. I had learned from previous experiences that when I withheld something from another person, I was selfish, and God would punish me. Even though that was what I thought I should feel, I could not shake this inner feeling that I did not want to become bitter because of those experiences. I wanted to be kind and beautiful. I began to see that beauty is what beauty does—which, to me, signifies what comes from the heart and not physical appearances.

CHAPTER SIX

Finding an Escape

*P*atrick and I were in the silo throwing down silage (fodder) for the cows when he pulled out a small portable device. With relish, he showed me that it was a radio and explained how it worked. Basically, I had to turn the dial to get the station or style of music I wanted to listen to. Patrick informed me that country was the best and then showed me the numbers for those stations. This radio came with headphones. Before that day, I'd had no clue that headphones existed! I had never before held such a device, but I knew I enjoyed music. After listening to the radio, I realized I more than enjoyed it—I loved music almost as much as I loved reading. I was amazed that I could listen to music, and no one else could hear it. Patrick told me he would share his radio if I promised not to tell our parents. That was a no-brainer, and I immediately agreed to that deal.

Now that I knew a radio was around, I wanted access to it more often. I wanted to know where I could find it. Unfortunately, Patrick wasn't free to give me that information. The contraband radio belonged to Wilbur; therefore, Wilbur would have to tell me where it was stored.

One day, Wilbur showed me the hiding place. It happened to be on his buggy in a secret compartment only a few people knew about. I was told only to use it when our parents and younger siblings weren't around to catch me accidentally. Once I knew of the radio and demonstrated I was willing to keep the secret, I was allowed to be part of the older siblings' group more often.

Upon joining ranks with my five older siblings, I was permitted to help them play card games on our in-between Sundays—the Sundays that we did not have church. One game we frequently played was Rook. This is a gambling card game and not one our church would have allowed had they known about it. However, they never found out, as we only played it in the secret of one of my older siblings' rooms. My parents knew we played the game, but as long as we kept it upstairs and not in the family room downstairs, they turned a blind eye.

We typically played four-person Rook. Although we did not use money in our games, that did not make it any less serious. When I was first introduced to the game, I was far from an expert. In fact, I struggled to hold my own. However, after being lectured on my inabilities or lousiness a few times, I learned to memorize all the cards as they were played in any particular round. I had to know what was already played, especially if I happened to be partners with Wilbur. Making a mistake during the game was unacceptable. I was super competitive, and remembering the cards played helped my overall chances of winning both the card game and Wilbur's approval.

I was always trying to gain Wilbur's approval, hoping he would stop molesting me. I thought he was targeting me because he hated me. Nothing seemed to make him like me enough to end the abuse.

The summer I was twelve, I had the privilege of staying with my out-of-state grandparents for ten days. This was a big deal for me; I had never been away from my family for any period of time, let alone out of state.

At first, I was nervous when I realized that my boy cousins who lived next door wanted to interact. I had developed a mistrust for males of every kind, always expecting the worst from each one. I felt unsafe, regardless of who the male was, but that summer, with the boys' persistence, I finally caved and started visiting with them. As my stay progressed, I began watching the boys' actions and really taking note of how they treated me. In turn, I started asking myself, *Do I feel safe with this male? If so, why?* Ultimately, I learned a very valuable lesson: not every male will mistreat me. Accordingly, I started focusing on how I was treated or how the male made me feel when I was in their vicinity.

All in all, I had the opportunity to spend time with many of my cousins whom I hadn't really known until that summer. I ended up having a great experience staying with my grandparents and traveling around to the different extended families in the community.

While in the area, I found out that two of my cousins were planning to be married in a few weeks, and I was excited for them. However, I had only been home for a short while when the invitation for the weddings arrived. With this much-anticipated piece of mail came the realization that most—but not all—of my family would attend the weddings. I immediately understood a couple of things: one, I would not be able to have another trip that summer because I had already had my turn; and two, I would be in for it if Wilbur stayed at home too. The weddings were to take place during the middle of strawberry season, and someone had to stay home to deal with chores and strawberries. The privilege I had so enjoyed now transformed into a nightmare. I knew I had to find a way to protect myself as the only girl staying at home with my two older brothers to do chores and take care of the strawberries.

My first line of action was to ask my closest friend to spend the night with me, as her brother was going to come help us do chores anyway. I pleaded with her to get permission to stay over, but it was to no avail. Her parents wouldn't agree.

My next tactic was to go to bed before my brothers in hopes I could be sleeping before Wilbur came upstairs. Maybe that would save me. Unfortunately, I soon found out that wouldn't work. Although I went to bed early, I could not for the life of me fall asleep. When my brothers came upstairs to go to bed, I decided to pretend to be sleeping anyway. They went to their own rooms, but soon, I heard Wilbur enter mine. He came to my bedside and asked me to come to his room in a few minutes so that Patrick had time to fall asleep first. Still feigning slumber, I ignored him, but when he left, he insisted, "Come to my bed soon."

I was terrified. What could I do? It never entered my mind to go lock my door, which would not have helped as Wilbur had a key anyway. I lay there paralyzed. What would happen now? I had no intention of going to Wilbur's bed!

After some time, I heard Wilbur approaching my room again. I knew I was trapped with no way out. He would have his way, regardless of how hard I resisted. Although I pretended to be sleeping again, Wilbur climbed into my bed and started touching me. I tried to fight him off, but I simply wasn't strong enough. Wilbur proceeded to wear me out. Then, he covered me with his body and rubbed my vagina with his penis until he was satisfied. When he left, I lay there crying, having no energy and possessing a smoldering resentment toward myself for not being stronger. I knew I needed to get up and clean myself. However, for a while, I was too consumed by hopelessness and despair to even move.

I soon realized this was going to happen every night until my family came home at the end of the week. It was one of the longest and blackest periods of my life at the time. I had not known such darkness, such hell. No matter what I did, Wilbur would have his way with me. There was nothing I could do to prevent it from happening.

When my family finally returned, I was overjoyed to see them. Even though Wilbur still found ways to corner me, I took solace in the fact that at least it would not be every night. I had made it through the worst of it and clung to the hope that things might get better soon.

At twelve, I had seen some dark times and found refuge in prayer by accident. I only knew a little about this common practice, but it was a tradition in our home to recite family prayer after morning and evening meals. On one such occasion, I found myself uttering in agony this plea: "Please, Lord, make my brother stop hurting me." After this, when we knelt for prayer, I did not hear my dad's words anymore; instead, I focused on talking to God, expressing my feelings about my family situation, and pleading with Him for help.

My natural situation had not changed, but I no longer felt alone. I started to pray daily, sometimes constantly. I realized I did not have to be on bended knee to pray but could have a prayerful heart, no matter where I was or who was with me. I found myself talking to God, telling Him of my pain and asking for His help. I repeatedly prayed, "Please, God, make it stop! I know you can. You are God. You are all-powerful and can do anything you want, so please stop the pain!"

God heard my cry, and He asked me to talk to an adult about what was happening, but I couldn't figure out who to tell. So in prayer, I asked God, "Who am I to tell about the situation?" I went through my entire adult family, asking God, "Should I talk to this one?" But I kept getting a no—until, eventually, our non-Amish neighbor's name came to me.

The thought of approaching this neighbor terrified me. It was so beyond my comprehension that I immediately wanted to dismiss it. Somehow, I knew if I spoke to her about it, she'd get help, but what would happen if someone from the outside found out? Wouldn't that make my family look bad? I just wanted Wilbur to stop hurting me and my sisters—I didn't want to destroy my family. I had been taught that to be right with God, I had to obey my parents, and while I had not asked them, I was sure they would not want me to talk to my neighbor about this. I argued in my spirit about what to do, and in the end, I didn't listen to God's direction.

Although I continued to live in fear and pray for deliverance, I didn't have the faith to actually take the action that could deliver me from my painful environment. I had put conditions on how God could help me. I would only accept that God's voice was directing me if it fit into the rules I had been taught. Thus, life continued, and my situation didn't change. I had yet to learn that God is not a respecter of persons, and when He asks something of me, it is for my good, regardless of what I or others may think.

One afternoon, when I was thirteen, I was preparing to make ice cream for supper. Homemade ice cream and cake were frequent suppers in our family. I needed to find the sledge-hammer to smash the ice, so I went searching for it. For once, I was not paying attention to my surroundings as I entered the barn, which was unusual for me and cost me dearly. To my utter dismay, I was grabbed by Wilbur and forced to the hayloft. No matter how hard I fought, I was never physically strong enough to escape. I knew what was coming, and my spirit cried out, *GOD, PLEASE HELP ME!*

Wilbur lay me down on the hay mound floor, pulled up my dress, unbuttoned his pants, and covered my body with his. Then, all of a sudden, the strangest thing happened to me. I found myself hovering above Wilbur's back. I hung there looking down as he used my body as he wanted, but I could not feel anything that was happening to me. That's when I realized my spirit was not in my body. It was watching the scene unfold from above. I could only see my face, and as I gazed down from my position above my brother's back, the eyes that stared up at me looked hollow and dead. Empty.

When my brother was done, he stood and buttoned his pants. Still gazing down from my lofty position, I watched as my body lay there, unresponsive and exposed. I was simultaneously humiliated and angry toward my still body. Why didn't I move and get covered up? But my body didn't stir. Wilbur put my dress back down and reached his hand out for me, but still, my body didn't move. He then reached down and took ahold of my hand, and at that point, my spirit reentered my body. With Wilbur's help, I finally stood up. With no hint of regret for the horror he had just put me through for the umpteenth time, he dusted the hay and straw from my clothes and told me I could go now.

I was in a daze! What had just happened to me? How was it even possible for that to occur? Even though I did not understand any part of it, I knew without a shadow of a doubt that it was God's handiwork. I had been spared from something, even though I didn't know exactly what.

My mind spinning wildly, I went back to making ice cream. However, before I could get started, I experienced a wave of shock when I saw blood as I sat down on the bucket to crank/freeze the ice cream. There was blood on my dress, but where had it come from? I was very embarrassed. At first, I thought I had started my period. Pink-faced, I tucked my blood-stained dress under me so no one else would see it until I could take care of it. When I was done freezing the ice cream, I went to care for myself only to find out that I didn't have my period. I was puzzled. Where had the blood come from?

After this, it came to the point that when my brother tracked me down, I no longer bothered resisting him. The quicker I allowed him his pleasure, the sooner I was released. I no longer felt anything when he "played" with me. I had learned to detach my feelings from his touches and shove them behind an emotional steel wall inside my head. This was the only way for me to protect myself at the time.

As I write this, I am literally gagging and asking myself *why? Why didn't I fight and scream bloody murder every single time? Why didn't I kick him where it would have genuinely hurt him?* Sadly enough, I know why. My teenage self was lost and broken. I was not in a healthy state of mind where Wilbur was concerned. I had been overpowered for seven long years. The ongoing torture had transpired so many times that I no longer had any hope of escape.

At one point, when I was eleven, Wilbur promised me, "This is the last time. Just one more time." The first time he made that promise, I was overjoyed. There was renewed hope. But then, he did it again…and again and again. "What about your promise?" I asked him, but he just said, "Yes, I know, but this will be the last time." Yet it was never the last time, and my hope that he would truly stop wholly vanished. I no longer hated Wilbur; I just hated myself.

Desperate for reprieve, I started to read books to escape my misery. I would peruse anything I could get my hands on, which were Wilbur's romance novels. I knew not to let Mom or Wilbur catch me with these books, so I read through the night when everyone else was asleep. Many a night, I stayed up until the wee hours of the morning to finish a story. When I read, I escaped into a world where my problems did not exist. It was my only relief.

One Sunday afternoon, I lingered upstairs in my room after finishing another novel. I sat there thinking about my life, wondering where it would take me. Why did I have to be Amish? Why was I born into a family that only hurt me? Why could my brother not be like the brothers I read about in my books? A brother who was a protector of his sisters instead of someone causing me to need a protecter? I wished I had been born into a different family and different circumstances. If only my parents had decided to leave the Amish—that would surely have improved my life, wouldn't it? I recognized that these thoughts were unhealthy, but I didn't know how to deal with my suffering. I only learned to blame myself if things didn't go well. I didn't know how to actually fix anything.

I asked myself, *Will I always be Amish, or will I do what I've heard of only in whispers from my mom and older sisters? Will I leave the Amish for a different or funny belief one day?* (Somehow, I knew if I ever left the Amish, it would be because I didn't believe in the Amish religion anymore; otherwise, it would not be worth losing my soul.) Incidentally, we had just heard of a family from a neighboring community that had not only one but three children who had left the Amish for a funny faith.

In our community, a funny religion consisted of any belief that wasn't Amish. It was perceived to be better to leave the Amish strictly because of rebellion than to leave to pursue another religion. Overall, leaving the Amish was a grave sin, especially if one practiced another religion after one had been baptized. Then, the soul was considered damned for all eternity. However, if the person returned to the Amish before they died, there was hope for salvation.

Oh, how I longed for escape. Despite the desolation of my physical environment, I found some joy in the thought that it wouldn't be like this forever. Someday, I would be free and be with God if I remained obedient to my parents. I didn't fight with anyone if possible, and I didn't argue with Mom if she wanted to "fix" my head covering—aka make it as sloppy as possible. If I stood up for myself, it always meant some confrontation, so I tried to avoid it at all costs. I was afraid of jeopardizing my soul if I did not readily agree with everyone.

Ignoring was my choice of action when dealing with hurt or pain inflicted. I even started making excuses about why it was okay for me to be mistreated by my family and loved ones. My thought was I must have done something terrible for God to punish me. As a result, I was constantly looking for a way to redeem myself. I also felt that if I acknowledged the pain, the wall I had in place would crumble, and if that happened, it would destroy me, so I continued to ignore it.

One day, when I was fourteen, Wilbur asked me to follow him, as he had a secret to tell me. After he had used me and my spirit had returned to my body, he shared that he was getting married in a few months. I knew I should be happy for him, but I was only happy for myself, thinking I would finally be free from him. At the same time, I felt bad for his future wife. What would she have to endure from my brother who I knew was a monster?

CHAPTER SEVEN

Adjusting to a New Community

*W*hen I was sixteen, my family once again planned to relocate. My parents asked the four oldest children living at home for our thoughts on what community we would like to move to. They also talked with my married siblings about it. Bertha and Wilbur and their families lived in the same community. Of course, they wanted the grandparents to be around, making that community more appealing to my parents. I was not too fond of the idea of living in the same area as Wilbur. Not only was he finally out of the home, but he was also in a different neighborhood, and I desperately wanted it to stay that way.

I wanted to move to a community where we had no prior ties. Magdalena was planning her wedding then and didn't care; she knew the community she was moving to after her wedding was not one my parents would consider. Patrick's girlfriend, Susie, was a schoolteacher in the same area that Bertha and Wilbur lived in, so that was his vote. In the end, much to my dismay, it was decided we would move to that community.

That summer and fall, my sister Melissa and I were in charge of the farm while my parents started construction on the new farm. My family bought 120 acres of bare land, and we started building from the bottom up. We decided to construct the barn and start on the house before we moved. That summer was the best part of my life while living with my family. Even though it was a lot of hard work, I loved my life on the farm again. This was the first time in a long time that I felt safe at home. Wilbur was out of the house—and the community for that matter—and my parents weren't around to find fault with me. I could live freely and breathe deeply without fear of any kind being present.

With no parents around, it was the perfect time to have a radio. When I mentioned this to one of our non-Amish neighbors, they went out and bought one for me. I used it every day, listening to country music while doing my daily chores. I became very resourceful in finding ways to use my radio, even with little ones around. I even listened to it when my parents returned to help with the packing and moving process. I had gotten very comfortable using the radio regardless of who was in the vicinity, as it was easy to hide earbuds with my scarf/head covering. Plus, I discovered that when I had the music turned down low, I could still hear when someone was talking to me without creating suspicion.

I knew I wasn't supposed to have a radio, so I decided not to take it with me to the new home. Once we moved, I wanted to start with a clean slate and follow the rules completely; maybe that would make my life more peaceful.

At this point, I was almost seventeen, the age I would join the youth group. I dreaded the thought of being a part of the youngie. I did not like the idea of dating. I was a plain girl with terrible secrets; no one else should have to deal with them. Yet I had already made this decision in my heart: if I ever dated and thought I wanted to marry him someday, I would tell him about my past. I could never marry someone who didn't know about my history before he had to spend the rest of his life with me.

We moved in late fall, and winter was upon us before we could make residence in the main house. So we lived in the basement for the first six months while working on finishing the rest of the house. While living in the basement, we put the washing machine outside on the cement porch. As you can imagine, it was a bit "chilly" doing laundry that first winter. Having to hang the laundry out in the cold was familiar, but doing the actual washing in the cold was unusual for us, and it made laundry day very unpleasant.

Life in our new location was better than I thought it might be. Bertha knew I wasn't thrilled that Mom and Dad had chosen this community, so she was trying to highlight the good in that decision by helping me find new friends, including a girl named Elsie. Bertha had high praise for her family; they had moved there a year before us. She thought Elsie would make the perfect friend for me, and from the stories she told me, I felt like I knew her already. Bertha said, "Elsie is friendly and outgoing to everyone; it's as if she meets no strangers." This girl did no wrong, according to Bertha, and in turn, I had high expectations of her.

Betty, Elsie's older sister, and Linda were Bertha's good friends. Linda was married, but her family lived in our community too, and she had a younger sister named Lydia. Come to find out, Lydia's brother Matt and Elsie's sister Meredith were married and had left the Amish church two years before I ever met the girls. These were the families I had heard my older sisters and mom whispering about when their children had left for a funny belief a few years ago. This had caused a great uproar in the two communities Matt and Meredith had left.

This kind of news is like a rock when it hits the water. The initial splash soaks everyone close to the situation, and the waves roll outward, hitting the surrounding communities individually. Unlike the natural ripples, these never seem to stop; the tides still leave their mark years later. Having this experience in common and Elsie dating Lydia's brother Peter helped the two girls become close friends. I had met Lydia before, and now that I'd heard such an enthusiastic endorsement from Bertha, I was very excited to meet Elsie too.

Neither of these families were in our church district. However, the family hosting church in our district was good friends with Lydia's family. So I expected to see Lydia at church, and because she and Elsie were super close, I expected Elsie to be there too. Sure enough, both of the girls were present. When I spotted Elsie, I recognized her immediately based on Bertha's description. I was eager to meet this friendly, outgoing, and caring person. Why was I suddenly feeling bashful? I had not expected the extreme insecurity I felt when seeing her.

Lydia knew both of us, so I expected her to make the introductions, although looking back now, I'm not sure why, as introductions were not typical in our culture. When it didn't happen before church services began, I thought it would happen after services as we girls sat around waiting for lunch. However, as it turned out, Elsie and Lydia had been asked to help serve lunch.

Afterward, when the youngie were leaving for home, I realized that I would only meet this amazing Elsie if I made the first move. I wasn't usually so shy around other girls. However, although I was used to my plainness, when I saw Elsie, I was immediately intimidated by her natural beauty. I had come to terms with my perceived lack of beauty, and when I realized that true beauty comes from the heart, I desired to be kind over beautiful. Holding that sentiment in my mind, I went to greet Elsie.

When I introduced myself, Elsie was friendly and admitted she knew who I was but hadn't gotten around to saying hi. Despite my high anticipation leading up to meeting Elsie, the reality was a bit of a letdown. Although I had finally met this amazing girl, I was greatly disappointed; instead of finding a friend, I felt unworthy of her friendship.

I liked Elsie but wondered why she didn't like me. Why had she not found the time to approach me, especially after it had been reported that she greeted everyone with a welcoming smile? Years later, I talked to Elsie about this and discovered she was just as insecure about herself when she met me as I was about her. Interestingly, we both allowed our natural appearances to change our actions toward the other. Typically, we were both kind, outgoing girls. However, as I've gone through life, I've come to understand that insecurities reveal themselves when someone else does or says something we wish to keep hidden, and often, it's done in total innocence. I'm happy to say that despite our rocky start, Elsie was someone I grew to appreciate in many ways.

A few weeks later, on Old Christmas, a holiday the Amish uphold, I had the privilege of getting to know Elsie a little better. Old Christmas consisted of fasting (for the church members or baptized ones) and resting for the whole family, and it was a no-work day, regardless of what day of the week it fell on. Traditionally, instead of completing chores, we would visit with each other after lunch. On this occasion, Lydia's family had invited our family to join them to spend time with Elsie's family as well. It was a way for us to show our support regarding the loss of their children to the outside world.

We arrived at Elsie's home, and after she, Lydia, Susie, and I had mingled for a while, the other three girls decided to invite the four older boys to join us for some card games. There were four girls and four boys in the room, and two of the four girls and boys were dating each other, so it was easy to understand why they wanted to hang out together. However, being around single boys made me very uncomfortable. On the bright side, with the four boys joining us for games, we had the perfect setup to play Dutch Blitz, a fast-paced card game, as teams.

The boys came into Elsie's room as a group, but for a moment, I only noticed one of them. Who was he? I typically did not notice guys, but this one immediately drew my eye. As introductions were made, I found out this was Mike, Elsie's younger brother. I had an immediate crush on Mike, which made me very uncomfortable, unease settling in my stomach even as my heart skipped a beat or two. I did not want to do anything that would reveal my feelings—how I wished I were anywhere but in that room getting ready to play a card game with him. I felt the more I was in Mike's presence, the more likely I was to reveal my feelings unintentionally.

CHAPTER EIGHT

My Life as an Amish Teenager

I started attending the Sunday night youth group with Patrick and Susie. Once a girl began with the youngie, she would ride with her brother if she had one, or a neighbor boy would offer her a ride to and from the youth group. I was fortunate to have an older brother whom I could ride with.

The youth group activities consisted of weekly Sunday night gatherings at 7:00 p.m. when supper was provided. If not, the meeting would start between 7:30 p.m. and 8:00 p.m. There would be one and a half to two hours of group singing, followed by some visiting time before everyone returned home. If a boy wanted to go on a date with a girl, this was the time that would happen.

A typical date was a buggy ride from youth group to the girl's home. (This was one reason why the girls didn't use their own transportation.) After that, the couple would sit in the dark for an hour or two, trying to get to know each other. The length of the buggy ride depended on the time left over for visiting. The boy was supposed to leave by 1 a.m. If the couple decided to pursue a friendship, they would continue to have a date every two weeks for the next couple of months. Once they got that far, they would be considered a couple. Then, the boy would start picking up the girl and taking her to youth group as well.

It was Sunday evening, and my parents were gone for a weekend trip to another community. When I was preparing for youth group, I began to feel uneasy. I wanted to stay home, and I couldn't help but wonder if those feelings were a warning of some kind. When I asked Melissa if she was comfortable being the oldest at home until Patrick and I returned, she said she felt fine and encouraged me to enjoy myself. With Melissa's reassurance, my unease lifted, and I left for the evening.

I had made some casual friends and enjoyed seeing them every Sunday night. However, as we sat down to start singing, my feeling of unease returned. Afterward, we girls were hanging out in the basement when a girl named Kristine came up to me and asked for a private word. Nonplussed, I followed her to a remote location, and she asked me for a date on behalf of her cousin. Utterly blindsided, I gave her the first response that came to my mind: nope.

She left to relay the answer, and I tried to gather my wits about me. I wanted to join the group again but did not want to show any of my sudden awkwardness. However, before

I could rejoin the group, Kristine returned, asking why my answer was no. Her cousin wanted to know. What was I supposed to say? I was too nervous—but I couldn't say that. So I avoided the question altogether and went with the excuse that my parents were not home that evening, which meant we would not have any chaperones, yet we were required to have chaperones in the house when we had a date.

Although it only happened a few more times, I was never again surprised when asked for a date because I always got the same unshakeable feeling of dread before heading to the youth group.

Once we were settled in our new home, my parents decided to open a store. We obtained food that could no longer be sold through the regular retailers and sold it at a discount in our shop. For example, if a truck were hauling a load of canned goods and happened to be in a vehicle accident, causing some of the goods to be damaged, the whole truckload of supplies would have to go to a salvage warehouse. The goods that weren't damaged could go to bent and dent stores and be sold at a discount, but they were not allowed in the regular grocery stores. That's where our family's shop came in!

Our store had a customer area up front and a storage area in the back. We had just enough space to fit one semi-load of products into storage with the pallets stacked to the ceiling. At first, going through the boxes to see if we could find any interesting items was fun, and sometimes, we were lucky enough to find a radio or a camera. If Patrick discovered these things, he claimed them. If we found clear nail polish, we girls grabbed and used it, but it had to be done secretly, as nail polish was prohibited. This continued until our parents realized what was happening. Then, we could not rummage through the boxes until Mom had gone through them first.

After some trial and error, we all found our place in the system. Mom went through the boxes to clean and price items, while Melissa, SaraAnn, and I took turns shelving and caring for the customers. Dad's job was to ensure we had enough supplies.

Melissa did not enjoy working in the store, so as time went on, she took over the daily running of the household while SaraAnn and I filled in where we were needed between the store and the house. Meanwhile, Mom was in the store every day except Sunday.

Our shop offered a variety of food and beauty products. We did not get to pick the products; we simply sold what was sent to us. In addition, we had every candy you could think of—an added attraction to entice our nieces and nephews to come to Grandpa's house.

It didn't help matters that the oldest nephew, Joseph, was only six weeks younger than my youngest sister, and they liked to play together. Sometimes, Joseph would sneak across the road and come to Grandpa's house without telling his mom. It was a busy road with many curves, so we were quite alarmed the first time he showed up alone—though his mom arrived soon after. When Joseph was asked,

"Where is your mom?" he replied proudly, "At home. I came by myself." He was only three years old at the time.

Having Bertha live so nearby was a joy for me. She had married and left home before I was old enough to get to know her. Now that I was older, she trusted me and would confide in me about some things. We discussed different topics, mainly the church problems coming her way because her head covering and clothes were too neat and the drama between her and her three closest friends.

Sometimes, the talk included who was "that way again," meaning pregnant, and how soon the gal had become pregnant after her last pregnancy. Naturally, there was a lot of comparison among young women, and pregnancy was no exception. The younger married women in the church were always on the lookout for who was expecting but trying to hide it for as long as possible.

I was always embarrassed to hear the ladies talk about who was pregnant. I felt dirty thinking about how the pregnancy had happened, which I had found out through the books I read. Sometimes, I wonder if Mom sensed my discomfort on this topic, and maybe that is why she never talked to me about pregnancy and conception.

It was no small feat to hide your early pregnancy with everyone constantly looking for tell-tale signs. Bottle feeding your baby was a sure indicator that you were with child. Breastfeeding was the only "birth control" allowed, so one did not stop breastfeeding unless they were pregnant again.

Therefore, everyone who was keeping tabs knew what had happened, making pregnancy seem shameful. As a result, having children was not necessarily a blessing anymore.

As I mentioned previously, I had not wanted to live in the same community as Wilbur, for I still feared him. Even though he had not molested me since getting married three years prior, I still didn't feel safe in his presence. However, the more I got to interact with my nieces and nephews—both Wilbur's and Bertha's children—the more I came to appreciate having them around. I found comfort when interacting with little ones, my younger siblings included. At the time, I did not realize why I loved children so much, but knowing what I do now, I realize it was because of their innocence. I could give them love, and they would not only receive it gladly, but they would give it back without any extra requests.

In springtime, when I was seventeen, my parents instructed me to take baptism classes to join the church. I was not ready to be baptized, but I didn't have the nerve to disobey my parents. On Sunday morning, when the classes began, I followed the ministers out of the main church service area into a private space prepared for me and the three other young folks who were taking these classes as well. Once we got to the private room, the ministers started preparing us to be church members. Over the next twelve weeks, on a biweekly basis, we continued to follow this routine and learn more about our religion, what it meant to be Amish, and what would be expected from us once we were baptized church members.

Two weeks before baptism day, a concern was brought to the ministers regarding whether I could be baptized. Evidently, my head covering was not within the ordnung. This came from another church member, and I found out who with some digging. Once I knew who had complained, I approached her after church services and asked her what was wrong with my head covering. She said, "It is much nicer than I can get mine and still be in the ordnung." I was surprised! Because another woman was jealous of my head covering, my integrity in the church had been questioned. How did that have anything to do with my faithfulness? I had worn the same head covering throughout the summer, and now, just before I was baptized, it was no longer in ordnung?

When the bishop found out it was the same head covering I had worn all summer, he voted in my favor. Despite this small "victory," this incident showed me how vulnerable I would be once I was baptized. At the same time, I experienced a strange dichotomy. On the one hand, I didn't even want to be baptized, yet when the church questioned my faithfulness, I wanted to prove that I *was* faithful. Ultimately, I completed the classes and was deemed fit to become a true church member. Thus, I was officially baptized into the church.

CHAPTER NINE

Confession

It was early summer, the time of year it was fun to go for an open buggy ride in the evenings. During the summer, after evening chores, we were allowed to drive without our outer bonnets. This made everything look prettier, as there was nothing to hinder my view. However, on this particular evening, I was not enjoying the ride. Patrick, Susie, and I were on our way to the youth group, and I felt uneasy again.

When we got to our destination, Elsie and Lydia started acting strange. They kept looking at me and whispering to each other as if they knew something about me. I had gotten that familiar feeling before heading to singing, and because of their peculiar behavior, I was sure Mike would ask me for a date. This made me sad, for I felt if that were the case, it would be at my expense and not because he was truly interested in starting a relationship with me.

When it was time to head home, I was relieved once I stepped on the buggy, thinking, *Yes, I was wrong this time.*

However, after I took my seat, Patrick asked me, "Do you want a date with Mike tonight?"

"No way," I swiftly replied.

Surprised, Patrick said, "That's not very fair of you. You have given any other guy at least one date. Why not Mike?"

"Because I don't want to," I said, but both Patrick and Susie protested my response, encouraging me to change my mind. In the end, I realized I was trying to protect myself by saying no and decided, *So what?* If Mike wasn't serious by asking for a date, then I would handle it. So I ultimately agreed. With great trepidation, I climbed on Mike's buggy, wondering, *Why is he doing this?* I could not shake the feeling that he was having a good laugh, just doing what someone else had suggested.

News of my date with Mike spread quickly. My family had been expecting me to date him if I got the chance, so they weren't shocked. Apparently, my crush on Mike had not gone unnoticed by those closest to me. I tried telling Bertha and Melissa that I felt it was a trick date instead of a serious one, but they would not believe me. Nor would the rest of my family when they started asking questions after two weeks went by and Mike hadn't requested the expected second date. Some were happy that Mike didn't seem interested in pursuing another date, while others seemed confused. As for me, I just wished it had never happened. I was far too serious about the whole dating thing to be able to enjoy a date just for the fun of it.

I was tired of the whole dating thing, even though I had not been in the system for long. To me, dating should have more depth; it wasn't just fun. I was too serious and concerned about my future to take dating lightly. After the date with Mike, I prayed earnestly that if I were meant to find a partner, God would send the right guy my way. I knew he would be the one for me if he loved God more than the church's rules. Even though this did not make sense to me, as I was a rule follower, I believed this "knowing" that was coming from within.

Six weeks later, Patrick was extraordinarily slow in picking up me and Susie after singing. All the other girls had already gone home when he finally arrived. As we headed out the driveway, Patrick asked me, "Do you want to go on another date with Mike?"

Not sure if he was only teasing me, I retorted, "Don't you wish you knew?"

Patrick replied, "No, I'm serious. Mike asked for another date with you tonight. What do you say?" This time, Patrick did not have to persuade me to say yes.

Patrick and Mike had arranged to meet at a specific driveway if I agreed to the date. Patrick dropped me off there, and Mike picked me up. This time, my heart was glad as I climbed up onto Mike's buggy, for I knew he was serious now.

On our third date, Mike asked me if I would consider going steady with him. He was sincere and wanted to pursue a more permanent relationship with me. Yes, I wanted to pursue a relationship with him too, but first, I needed to know why things had gone the way they had initially.

With candor, he told me the first date had been just for fun. Apparently, he had jokingly said he wanted to go on as many dates as possible, and when Lydia had suggested that he ask me for one, he had said, "Sure, why not? I have to start with someone."

While this aligned with what I had felt, I needed more details. So Mike elaborated, divulging the complete story. In a nutshell, it had been Lydia's idea for him to go on a date with me and "dump me," as I had dumped all (two) other boys. A little hurt and confused that Lydia continued flirting with him while dating his best friend Joel, Mike was happy to comply with her suggestion. In conclusion, he said, "Because you were kind, even though I knew I was playing a trick on you, the trick lost its appeal, and I started thinking of you in a different light over time."

Mom was unhappy when my parents discovered I was pursuing a relationship with Mike, primarily because many of his siblings had already left the Amish. During one conversation with Mom about this, I told her, "While I am aware that half of his siblings have left the Amish, the more I'm learning about Mike, the more I recognize that he loves God, and that is what matters to me." Fortunately, Mom respected me in this and stopped admonishing me on that subject.

In September, Elsie and Peter were getting married. In the Amish culture, weddings take place at the girl's family home. The couple announces their engagement in church two weeks before the wedding date, and the next fortnight is busy with wedding preparations—deep cleaning, food prepping, and confirmation of helpers, among other things. In addition, two couples are asked to be part of the wedding party as witnesses. Mike was planning to be one of the witnesses and asked me to be his partner. The following two weeks were busy, and I found myself at Mike's home a few times, helping with preparations as the big day came closer.

The night before the wedding, the main party planned to meet at Elsie's home. After evening chores, Mike came to pick me up—the first time he had done so. I left with him, and we had an enjoyable trip back to his home. Lydia and Joel were already there when we arrived, and everyone's spirits were high. The rest of the wedding party waved merrily from the windows as we drove in. Mike decided to have fun with them, so after we parked by the barn, he jumped off the buggy, went to the back, pulled out a siren, and started blowing it. I was still on board, laughing at all the action. Totally oblivious, neither Mike nor I thought about how the horse would react.

Things changed in the blink of an eye. The siren scared the horse, still hitched to the buggy, and it took off running. Mike sprinted behind us, trying to hop on unsuccessfully. The horse, buggy, and I went right into the front of the barn at top speed. Halfway through, I gathered my wits enough to reach for the reigns. As we approached the back barn door, which was closed, I tried to stop the horse, which only caused some skidding and sliding, but we were going too fast for the horse to halt. We slammed full force into the door and went right through it as if it weren't even there.

Once we hit the pasture area, the horse knew where she was going and picked up speed again. We went around a sharp corner in the fence, which we completely missed, and were heading for the back pasture when I finally got the horse under control and stopped her.

In the blink of an eye, Mike got on the buggy, took me into his arms, and just held me, asking if I was hurt. "No," I said breathlessly. "I am fine." Mike told me he had been terrified as we'd gone through the back barn door. He'd feared I would be "smoked" as the door came back down.

While l was a little disoriented, I was not hurt, and when I started replaying the whole scenario in my mind, I started laughing uncontrollably and could not stop. Mike did not think it was funny. He had been helpless, which he did not enjoy, especially since he had caused the horse's scare in the first place. With a chuckle, I told him it had simply been too wild a ride with no injuries for it not to be funny. Despite my lighthearted attitude toward the situation, Mike still did not see the humor in it.

We returned to the barn, where the family and wedding party awaited us. They had seen me disappear into the barn and rushed out to see the damage. Before they even arrived, they saw me heading for the back field, still on the buggy.

We unhitched the horse and then investigated what damage had been done in the barn. We were stunned to find very little destruction; the most significant thing was the skid marks on the cement floor from the horse's shoes as it had tried to stop. Nobody and nothing was hurt or broken, so there was plenty to be thankful for. With a soft smile, I told Mike that was enough excitement to last me for a while, and he agreed it was plenty for him too.

The following day, as we girls were finishing our dressing preparations, Mike and Peter walked into our room and started taking pictures. This startled me, as both the boys were baptized, and cameras or picture-taking were not allowed. Then, that afternoon, Peter, Mike, and I were back in the shed where the ceremony had taken place when Mike and Peter got out some cigarettes and started smoking them. After Peter left, Mike taught me how to smoke too. I was trying it for the first time when a young married guy walked in on us. I was sure we would be in trouble, but I discovered that this guy didn't care and would not report us to the ministers. All in all, I was having quite the wedding experience and wondered if this was typical behavior for the wedding party. It was my first time being in a wedding, so I didn't know one way or another.

Later that evening, before the visiting family left to return to their communities, Peter, Mike, Joel, and a few cousins brought a bottle of peppermint schnapps to share with me, Elsie, and Lydia. Another big surprise to me. I knew these girls were okay with all kinds of flirting, but I had never known them to even consider drinking alcohol or taking pictures. When would the other shoe drop? I didn't have to wait long.

A week later, when Mike came to visit, he told me I should talk to his dad (the bishop in my church) about confessing, as Lydia had reported us, even though she had participated in all the illicit activities as well. I could offer to confess on my own before it was reported to the other ministers, or the deacon would come around asking me to confess after they found out.

In the end, I decided to talk to the bishop about my involvement and ask to confess in church the following Sunday. He was embarrassed for me at having been caught in the middle of all the activities that had happened. He said, "I'm sorry you have to do this, as I'm sure you would never have done these things if Mike had not encouraged you to do them."

I was amazed by his high esteem for me. Yes, I was an excellent rule follower now, but I knew what I had done before I met Mike. This is how I found myself before the church confessing a few weeks after I was baptized.

CHAPTER TEN

Telling of Secrets

*M*ike and I had been dating for almost a year. At first, things had been rocky between me and my parents at the start of our relationship, but everything had evened out. The two of us were devoted to each other, and I knew the time had come for me to tell Mike about my past.

Despite my conviction that I needed to open up about what had happened to me, I dreaded this conversation. What if he decided to abandon our relationship after he found out? Regardless of his choice, I had to do the right thing before we were serious enough to discuss marriage. I knew that if he broke up with me afterward, that did not make me less of a person. It simply meant he was not the one God had intended for me to do life with.

Mike and I had come home from an out-of-state wedding for his family and were upstairs in Mike's room when I confided in him about my past. He was shocked! He had heard of stuff like that happening in some families but had never imagined it would hit that close to him. In a solemn tone, I gave him a pass to walk away from me with no hard feelings, but if he chose to stay, I had one condition—that it was not out of pity!

Bracingly, Mike said my past did not change his feelings about me, but he was horrified at my brother. "Did you tell your parents?" he asked.

"No," I admitted. "You're the first person I've mentioned it to."

If possible, he looked even more surprised. "They need to know to protect your younger sisters," he insisted.

I told him I was protecting them by not allowing them to be alone with Wilbur when possible. However, he ultimately convinced me I should not have to shoulder that burden on my own and that my parents should at least know about it. Finally, I agreed to talk to my mom about what I had gone through.

Mom was stunned when I told her about Wilbur's actions. To my deep dismay, her first response was, "You may never tell anyone else about it, especially not Mike." That was incredibly hurtful to me. When I'd confided in Mike, he had encouraged me to trust my parents. Her reply—telling me to hide it—made it even more shameful, and I felt like I had done wrong by simply acknowledging it. How I wished I had not ever told her.

Mom indicated she was sure Wilbur had made things right because he had confessed in the church and had included his "life's walk," meaning anything in his past that he might have done wrong. Basically, instead of confessing and repenting for the abuse he put me through, his confession was vague and all-inclusive without really mentioning any specifics. Sure, I knew that Wilbur had made that confession. But I also knew that it did not fix or change anything. He had confessed his sins many times, but it had never stopped him from continuing the abuse. I did not dare say this to Mom, for her response had made me lose what little renewed hope I had felt when Mike had encouraged me to talk to my parents. A part of me had clung to the belief that maybe she would help me—but no, her only priority was to make sure no one else discovered this horrific secret about our family. Meanwhile, I was no longer sure that secrecy was the correct answer or solution.

Contrary to my initial fears, sharing my past with Mike strengthened our bond. I trusted him and revealed deeper thoughts and concerns to him. He, in turn, trusted me and started talking about his family's situation. Mike began opening up about those who had left the Amish and how it made him feel knowing that he was being judged by the community because of his siblings' actions and found lacking before he even had a chance to make his own mistakes.

With all the judgment he was enduring, he came to a place where other people's thoughts of him no longer mattered. Because his siblings had left, he wanted to know the right decision for him, and he started asking questions concerning the church rules. He asked me, "What is more important to follow—the Amish rules or the Bible?" See, after reading the Bible, he had found that the two did not align.

It was terrifying to me that the church's rules might not match up with the Bible. If that were the case, following the church regulations would and could not save me. As a result, I felt a desperate need to find the truth of the matter. When I asked, "Mike, how do we find out what's true?" he said, "We need to read the Bible and pray about it."

So I started diligently perusing my Bible and praying to understand what I was reading. Slowly, without realizing it, I began believing in those words on the page, and I wanted to know how to apply them to my life. I was starting to see that there was much more to godly living and salvation than blindly following a set of church requirements. I was desperate to seek the truth, but I had no idea what that meant then. Nonetheless, above all else, I hoped to find God's truth.

One day, I found a bilingual Bible on our bookshelf. In my spare time, I read it in the privacy of my bedroom. The further I got with my reading, the more the church rules confused me. Why did they focus so much on worldly and materialistic things? The color of our dresses or clothing we could wear, the neatness of the head coverings, what type of tools the menfolk used for building, how the kitchens could be designed… It went on and on. But there was little focus on honesty, morals, and integrity.

I asked my folks about this, and they explained it this way: each community has its rules because there are many different ideas about right and wrong. That way, each family can move to the community with the rules aligning with their beliefs. It is not sinful to move around and shop for better laws, but it is considered sinful to do what you believe if it does not align with the rules of the church to which you belong.

"Why don't our rules emphasize morals and honesty and focus less on the natural things we use and wear?" I asked.

Dad answered, "Well, we want everyone to be honest, but we can't do anything to enforce honesty or morals because we can't see those things. It is much easier to see what one is wearing or using."

After I started posing these questions, my parents became very concerned about my devotion to the Amish. I had been so faithful in following the rules since my baptism. I had never questioned the rules before, so why now? Was dating Mike affecting my faithfulness to the church? These were some of the questions my parents had for me.

I quickly told them that Mike was not telling me what to do about my Amish faith—he only encouraged me to read my Bible and pray. Little did I know that this was a huge no-no! In fact, in their minds, that was one of the worst things he could do. Nothing I said took any of the blame off of Mike. They were sure he was at fault for my disobedience, and it was time for me to break up with him. I disagreed with that decision and ignored their wishes.

Looking back now, I can see that this was actually the beginning of the end. My good reputation with my family started to change. They no longer had positive things to say about me. Before, they always gave me high praise for caring about right and wrong and doing what was deemed "right," but now they said I did not care—that my proclamation for wanting to be godly was a lie. This was hard for me to accept, but I knew I could not change their minds. I was, in fact, doing everything that was wrong according to the church. If I wanted to be godly, I would continue to follow the church laws set for me instead of questioning them and reading my own Bible. Nonetheless, I believed I was doing what was good and right for me. My heart felt sure that I was following God's wishes by continuing on my current path.

CHAPTER ELEVEN

Christmas Shopping

*I*n the fall of 2005, I was told I would be the teacher for our school district. Anybody who had graduated from the eighth grade—the highest level of education among the Amish—could be a teacher. Although I enjoyed children, I did not want to be responsible for their education. But this was one battle that I lost, and as school started, I found myself teaching twenty-one students all the subjects that made up the curriculum for our school systems.

On December 14, about fifteen minutes before dismissal time, I looked out the window and glimpsed a visitor coming our way. A knot started to form in the pit of my stomach. When I double-checked, I instantly knew who the visitor was.

By the time he had taken care of his horse and entered the schoolhouse, I had dismissed the students for the day. The children thought it was cool that we had this particular visitor—the teacher's boyfriend. I was planning to spend the night with the family of one of my students that evening, so my siblings left for home immediately too.

Once everyone else had left, I asked Mike, "What has brought you to see me on this snowy afternoon?"

He rose from the bench he had been sitting on while waiting for the children to leave and walked over to where I stood looking out the window. Putting his arms around me, he replied, "I think you know, but I'll tell you anyway. I'm leaving the Amish in the morning."

My heart sank. "Mike, why could you not wait to leave until after the holidays?" I implored. "It's only two more weeks."

"I know, Rose, and I'm sorry to hurt you like this, but it is time for me to leave," Mike said.

Then, he asked me what my thoughts were on the Amish. I was honest with him—I did not know what to think anymore. The more I read my Bible, the more confident I was that the Amish religion wasn't based on God's word, but all my life, I had been taught that leaving the Amish meant damnation for my soul. It felt like I was being split in half. If I abandoned the faith and culture I grew up in, I would be leaving my family behind, but the bigger question was would my soul be in danger of damnation if I went? I wanted a definite answer before I made any significant decisions.

Mike said, "I understand and encourage you to continue to read the Bible and pray. With time, you will receive an answer."

We sat and visited for a while. As the light left the schoolhouse, I knew our time together was coming to an end—at least for now. Mike was more than just my boyfriend; he was my best friend. He had shown me what it meant to have a true companion. As we said our goodbyes, I felt the tears start to form, but I could not hurt Mike by revealing the depth of my feelings, so I forced them back. I was good at pushing back my emotions and putting them behind "the wall."

Mike gave me his phone number, then hitched up his horse and drove away. I watched numbly as he disappeared from view.

I wanted to sit down and cry, but I knew I could not allow the tears to start. Otherwise, who knew when they would stop? So instead of giving in to my desire to sit and pity myself, I gathered the stuff I needed for the night, filled the stove with wood, locked the schoolhouse, and started walking.

I was thankful for the opportunity to stroll by myself before meeting my student's family. As I strode through the snow, my thoughts were racing. *When will I see Mike again? How much more pain can I endure? What is the right choice for me? Should I leave the Amish or stay?*

That night, as I knelt to pray before going to bed, I couldn't find any words except, "Lord, help me." Once I settled under the covers, I finally allowed the tears to come and cried myself to sleep. I knew that as sure as the morning would come, so would changes for my life as I knew it.

The next morning, I woke to the sound of male voices. I recognized one as the father of the household I was residing in, but I wasn't sure who the other voice belonged to. I could not hear what was being said, but I did hear the concern in both of their voices, which infused me with alarm. What could have happened during the night to cause us to receive a visitor so early in the morning?

I got out of bed and slowly got dressed for the day, preparing myself for another heartache to hit me when I arrived downstairs. Even after I was dressed, I waited to go downstairs until the visiting voice left.

As I walked into the kitchen, I was greeted by the early scents of breakfast and a sense of sadness. I did not have long to wait for the news. A neighboring family had lost a new-born baby during the night. This family was also one that had four school age children whom I taught. I knew it was going to be a sad day at school.

I arrived at the school with a heavy heart, wondering, *How should I structure the day*? I had no idea how to support these hurting children if they showed up in the classroom that day. At first, we stuck to our usual morning routine. Then, we transitioned to practicing for the Christmas program. We had just begun when I realized that was a bad idea. Most of my students were having a hard time emotionally, struggling in sympathy with their friends' loss. Just seeing how hard they were all trying to make the best of the situation broke my heart.

I called a halt to the program practice, and after I had given the other children an option to either color some more Christmas pictures or finish up assignments form the previous day, I went to talk with a few of the older children who had lost their sibling in the night. At a complete loss for words, I simply sat beside them and asked what it was that I could do to help them through that day.

As I sat visiting with the older daughter, I realized the children had been given the choice to come to school or stay at home that day, and they had chosen school, as they hadn't wanted to miss out on practicing for the program. Now that she was at school, she wished she could be home but didn't want to hurt my feelings by asking if she could leave. This truly touched my heart. Here this little girl was hurting, and although her heart was broken, she was thinking of me too.

Although it was not customary to show this type of affection, I reached out and gave her a hug. I told her I supported her completely for wanting to be at home and that we would not practice the program again until after we had time to grieve for the loss of her baby brother. After I had sent off the little family, I took a few minutes to gather my tattered emotions before turning to resume my duties with the other children. I knew that day would forever be in my memory, and it still is, but I'm happy to say it's with fondness instead of regret now.

The next few days were incredibly emotional for the students in my classroom, but we all tried to be encouraging to one another as best we could, and in the end, we made it through an unspeakably difficult time together.

The Christmas program was an event where all the family members came to watch the students recite poems and act out plays that they had worked hard to learn by heart. Afterwards, there were gifts for each student and the teacher followed by a time for socializing while enjoying the delicious food that the parents had brought with them.

Three days before this event, I had some last-minute shopping to do, so it was decided that Mom, Bertha, Patrick, and I would go to Dubuque. After school, our taxi arrived, and we left for our destination. Often, we knew our drivers, and this time was no different. Before we left, I had decided to request to borrow the driver's phone to make a call, so I was watching for a chance to ask him without my mom or sister around.

Aldi was our first stop. We all went in and started loading up our carts. Mom was in front when we came to the checkout line, and I offered to take our groceries out to the car so she could stay and help Bertha. Mom thought that was a good idea, so I headed to the car as fast as possible to unload the cart.

While there, I took the opportunity to ask the driver if I could borrow his phone. When he said yes, I was a little embarrassed but told him I didn't know how to operate a phone. Fortunately, he obligingly dialed the number, then handed the phone to me as it started to ring. I knew I had very little time to talk, so when Mike answered, I swiftly told him where I was and said I wanted to speak with him. However, I now realized I would not be able to since Bertha and Mom were walking out of the store. I hung up and surreptitiously handed the phone back to the driver as Mom opened the back door to finish loading groceries.

We were heading for Walmart when the phone rang. The driver answered, and when Mike said who it was, the driver exclaimed his name out loud. Mom and Bertha immediately turned around in their seats to look at me, and I fervently wished I could melt into my seat. The temperature in the van felt like it had just dropped ten degrees. The driver knew Mike, so he talked with him for a few minutes before hanging up.

We still went to Walmart, but the tension was palpable. I went about my shopping, thinking we would all do our own thing and meet up at the check stand like usual, but I soon noticed that either Mom or Bertha was always right with me. Their paranoia made our trip take longer, and I did not understand it, but that was okay with me. I was in no rush to get back home. Finally, with our shopping complete, we headed for the checkout area.

As I stood before the check stand, I noticed this non-Amish guy beelining down the aisle toward us. I didn't think anything of it; there were lots of non-Amish guys around. I just sidestepped so he had more space to pass, but he kept coming straight toward me. In disbelief, I looked more closely at his face and realized it was Mike. OH MY GOODNESS! I could not believe my eyes. Now it made sense why

Mom and Bertha had stayed on my heels after the phone call—they had been afraid that Mike would show up, and apparently their fears had been warranted.

I was totally overjoyed to see Mike, but I was also very nervous. What was the point in seeing him in passing at a store with Mom and Bertha right there beside me, clearly demonstrating their displeasure with his arrival? I completely forgot about my Christmas shopping as Mike and I began moving toward the exit with Patrick beside us. We started talking, and I was so wrapped up in the joy of being reunited with my boyfriend that I completely forgot my stuff.

Mom was frantic, trying to prevent me from going out the doors with him. I brushed off her concern and kept walking. Mike said he would get his vehicle and come to pick me up at the entrance. Fortunately, Mom did not hear him say this, so when Mike and Patrick went out the door without me, she relaxed and returned to get our stuff. Meanwhile, I went outside to wait for Mike.

Mom exited Walmart just as Mike drove up with Patrick in the front seat. Mike rolled down his window to invite me to get into the van, but Mom asked me not to. I was undecided. *What should I do?* I wanted to go with Mike, but I didn't want to cause Mom pain. When Patrick saw Mom's panic, he exited the vehicle, and in an instant, I knew my next step. I hopped into the passenger seat, and we took off.

My original party had planned to go to Menards before returning home, so I told Mike we should head there, thinking we'd meet up with the others. We were on the way there when his phone rang. It was Patrick. It was as if a switch had been flipped in that short time frame; Patrick wanted to know where we were and what Mike was thinking, taking off with me like that. Unwilling to sacrifice his precious time with me, Mike told him we would see them at Menards. We had just arrived there and parked when Mike got another phone call. This time, I talked with Mom. She wanted to know where I was. I told her we were sitting in the Menards parking lot, waiting for them to finish shopping.

As we sat visiting, Mike had another brilliant idea. Why couldn't he drive me home? That way, we'd have more time to catch up. I was happy to accept his offer, and I told my family of our new plan the next time his phone rang. They did not like this, so they kept calling, asking if we were making our way home. We answered their calls a few more times, and after reassuring Mom that I was indeed coming home that night, we told them we would no longer pick up the phone for them.

The miles back to the community flew by. We were not ready to separate when we arrived in town, so we decided to park on a back road for a while before Mike took me home. We had only been parked for a short time when the phone rang again. We answered it, and this time, it was my dad. He wanted to know where we were.

"We thought you were bringing Rosanna home. Is that not true?" he asked.

"Yes, that's still the plan," Mike said.

Dad wouldn't give up that easily. "I know you left before the other party, and they are home now, so where are you?"

"I will bring her home when we are done visiting."

We lost all sense of time as we discussed Mike's life outside the Amish and what had happened in the community since he'd left. As we talked, I discovered that Mike had written to me, but I had never seen the letter. Since I was in school all day, my parents had seen his letter first and kept it from me.

Before I knew it, it was four in the morning. I was ecstatic to have this time with Mike, but now, it was time to go home. I was sure my parents would be waiting for me, and I still needed to get up for school in the morning, so Mike took me back to my house.

He waited in the driveway until I entered. Seeing his headlights leave, I wished with my whole being that I was still in the vehicle with him. But I wasn't, so I figured I may as well accept that and prepare myself for what was before me.

Sure enough, Mom and Dad were sitting in the living room waiting for me when I entered the house. I intended to head straight for the stairs, pretending nothing was out of the ordinary, but I was asked to sit down with them. I plopped down with a sigh. I knew full well that what I had done was not okay in any form if I was planning to be Amish. I wasn't sure if I would stay Amish or not, but I wasn't ready to acknowledge this to my parents.

"What was that stunt you pulled all about?" my dad demanded.

"What stunt?" I asked.

"You driving away with Mike and not coming home until now is unacceptable! You scared both your mom and your sister," Dad admonished me.

More than a little annoyed, I responded in a typically defiant fashion. "What's the big deal that I came home with Mike? Didn't you believe me when I said I was coming home?"

"Well, we heard that Mike said he was bringing you home, but when you weren't back when Mom got home, we weren't sure what to believe," Dad admitted.

"Okay, I can understand that," I said, "but didn't we tell you again after Mom was home that I was coming back?"

"Yes, but we were afraid you wouldn't," Dad replied. After this, I had nothing to say regardless of their question or concern, and soon, I was dismissed.

I went to bed and slept for a few hours before it was time to prepare for school. Prior to leaving, I asked Ferman, one of my younger brothers, if he would do me a favor. I had not given Mike his Christmas present before he had left the Amish, so the night before, I had asked him to stop by the next day and pick it up. Since I would be gone, I wondered if Ferman would give it to Mike on my behalf. Ferman said yes.

At school that day, we practiced one more time and finished the last-minute details of decorations and preparations for the Christmas program, which was happening the following day. While I was gone, Mike arrived at our house for his Christmas present. However, when my folks realized that Ferman was planning to give it to him, they forbade him to deliver it to Mike, insisting he no longer deserved that present. Ferman was caught between a rock and a hard spot, but in the end, he obeyed his parents.

I had a fun day at school with the children only to arrive home and discover that Mike had shown up and left again without his gift. When I asked my parents about this, I was informed that the present was no longer mine to give away. They had paid for it for me when Mike was still in good graces with the church, but they were now taking it back. I didn't deserve the privilege to gift it anymore if I planned to give it to Mike after he sinned by leaving the Amish.

I wasn't sure what to make of this, so I just left it. I knew we were heading toward a more significant standoff soon, but I wasn't ready. I knew in my heart that I didn't want to break up with Mike but that my parents' wishes and the church rules would demand I give up my relationship with Mike if he was not Amish anymore.

The following day, I had to be at school at eleven o'clock. It was the day of our program. With all our preparations done and the program set to start at one p.m., I decided to sleep in, then get up and wrap the presents I had purchased when Mike had showed up at Walmart.

I had worn some of my brother's white socks to bed the night before and was still sporting them when my dad arrived upstairs the following day as I was finishing up with the last packages. At first, I tried to ignore my dad's arrival by not acknowledging him and continuing with my present wrapping. But it was to no avail—I knew this would be a big confrontation when Dad pulled up a chair and sat in my doorway.

Dad started the conversation by asking why I was wearing white socks. Thankfully, I'd had time to process some of the things happening lately. I knew the church thought men wearing white socks was perfectly alright, but women wearing white socks was sinful. I could not support these kinds of rules anymore. So, when asked why I was wearing white socks when I knew that was not allowed in the church, I simply and honestly said, "Because I see no problem wearing white socks."

"Don't you have enough respect for the church to obey the rules?" Dad demanded.

"No, not for things like this anymore," I replied determinedly.

Dad then said that what I had done by coming home with Mike the other night would not be accepted. "You will have to break up with Mike until he decides to return to the Amish church and be reinstated as a law-abiding Amish person again."

"Says who?" I fired back.

"Mom and I," Dad replied firmly. "We talked about it and decided to treat you the same way we handled Bertha when her boyfriend—now husband—left the Amish while they were dating. She had to break up with him until he rejoined the Amish. The same rules are going to be applied to you," Dad said.

"That may have worked with Bertha, but I am not planning to break up with Mike anytime soon," I stubbornly insisted.

I had just used up the last of my wrapping paper, and after my statement, Dad picked up the empty cardboard roll, hit me across the head with it, and said, "You are going to obey or else."

"Or else what?" I countered defiantly. "You're going to beat me? Sorry—beat me all you want, but that will not make me change my mind."

Seeing that I would not move on that issue regardless of what he did, Dad left, stating that it wasn't over yet. I hated these kinds of confrontations, but I was not afraid anymore for some reason. For the first time in my life, I was standing for what I believed in without considering the cost.

CHAPTER TWELVE

Family Time Ends

*T*wo thousand and five was over. It was now January 1, 2006. New Year's Day landed on a Sunday, and it was our in-between Sunday to boot, so that meant I could sleep in. When I woke, it was to a gray overcast day. I awakened with a strange feeling in my heart. It was a peculiar feeling I had never had before, so I didn't know what to expect, but I knew enough to trust that something was about to happen.

With that sense of foreboding heavy in my stomach, I went downstairs to see what everyone was up to. They were all doing their typical in-between Sunday activities. Mom was reading in her rocking chair, and Dad was taking a morning nap. Melissa and Susie were in their rooms, and Patrick wasn't home. He had left with a non-Amish friend the night before and had not yet returned, which was unusual. The rest of the children were playing.

I was restless and asked Melissa if she'd join me on a walk. Side by side, we traipsed to the back fields on our farm.

As we walked and talked, I discovered Patrick had gone to a New Year's Eve party and still needed to show up at home. I realized I had been too immersed in my misery to pay much attention to the rest of my family around me.

When we returned from our walk, Mom wanted to know where we had been. I told her we had gone to the back of our property, but she wasn't satisfied with my answer. She asked me straight up, "Did you go call Mike?"

"No, I did not." I admitted that I had thought about it but had decided against it. Truth be told, I had finally gotten my answer about leaving the Amish, so I wanted to call Mike and talk to him about it, but I didn't give Mom those details.

Before it was time for them to leave, Patrick arrived home and took Melissa to the youth group as usual. Susie and I were finishing supper dishes when she asked me what I planned to do after we were done. I had intended to go to my room and be by myself (which I had been doing a lot lately when I was home), but instead of saying that, I asked her why she wanted to know. Evidently, she wanted to play games as a family and wondered if I would join them. Before I could answer her, the strange feeling from earlier came back stronger. The thought entered my mind that this could be my last night with the family, and I should spend time with them, so I accepted Susie's invitation.

With supper dishes done, the family gathered in the living room, preparing for a night of games. This was pretty typical for Sundays, as we were busy every other night of the week until bedtime. Sometimes, we played card games, but we decided to play dominoes that evening. The entire group relaxed as we got started, and for the first time in a long while, I enjoyed some family time again. Things had been so tense lately that I had forgotten to enjoy my family.

It was close to eight o'clock when there was a knock at the kitchen door. Mom looked at me as if I should know who it was, but I had no clue and shrugged my shoulders at her unspoken question. A moment later, the door opened, and Mike waltzed in. Wilbur and Malinda were right behind him with their two little boys. Oh boy! My heart leaped joyfully to see Mike again; however, my parents reacted differently.

Dad walked out to the kitchen toward Mike, asking, "What are you doing here?" Mike said he wanted to talk to me, but my dad kept forging forward and forced him to back right out the door again. In a menacing tone, he told him, "You are not welcome to date my daughter or come into this house again until you decide to rejoin the Amish church." I made eye contact with Mike before the door closed in his face, and I prayed that that was enough for Mike to see that I disagreed with my dad.

As Mike retreated, I did some fast thinking, knowing I had only a few seconds to make critical decisions. If I made a run for it out the back door, I might get out before my dad caught me, but I was barefoot, and it was the middle of winter. Or I could go to the basement, get my everyday clothes, and meet up with Mike outside. I would have to go through the kitchen to get to the stairs, and even if I made it down the inside stairs, my dad would probably meet me on the outside of the basement door. So I decided to go upstairs for my good (Sunday) coat and shoes and try to go outside afterward.

I was exiting my room fully dressed when I saw Dad start up the stairs. In a rush, I realized I had made the worse decision ever—now I was trapped! Dad immediately charged toward me, and I tried to go around him, but when he put his hand out to grab me, I saw he was ready for a fight. I was not about to give him any reason to touch me, so I retreated. Without missing a beat, he followed me to my room, wanting to know what I was planning to do.

"I want to go talk with Mike."

"NO," he immediately responded. "That is unacceptable unless Mike repents."

At that exact moment, I heard a loud truck pull into our driveway and back up to the front door. One of the siblings came upstairs to inform me that Mike was there, and he was asking for his bed.

Mike had given me a bed as a birthday present the week before he'd left the Amish. When he'd presented it to me, we'd both known it was only a matter of time before he left the Amish, so I'd asked him, "Why give me a bed when you are leaving soon anyway?" Mike had replied jokingly, "Well, maybe when I come for my bed, I can take you with me too." Those words had never left the secret of my heart, so when I heard that Mike was asking for the bed, I thought, *Maybe he is trying to tell me something*, but I was still pretty upset.

In stark contrast, Dad was thrilled to get rid of my bed. I was adamant that he couldn't just take it apart and give it away like that. However, when Wilbur came up and conveyed that Mike was asking for his bed back, they ignored my pleas and started dismantling it.

Thinking I might have a better chance to talk to Mike out the window if I was in Patrick's room, which was right above the front door, I left my room. At first, Dad wouldn't let me. With a sour look, I said that I didn't want to linger if they were giving away my birthday present against my wishes and that I was planning to go to Patrick's room. Only then did Dad allow me to leave his sight.

Meanwhile, Mike was locked out of the house with a person standing guard at each door. As Dad and Wilbur arrived with each part of my bed, they unlocked the door and opened it only enough to shove the piece of furniture through before the door was closed and locked again.

The more time passed, the more desperate I became. I feared Mike would leave after he had his bed before I had time to talk to him, and I *needed* to talk to him. I needed to tell him I was leaving the Amish the following weekend. I needed to make plans for him to pick me up. Unfortunately, the way things were going, that was not going to be possible. What was I going to do?

Mom had come into Patrick's bedroom just as I approached the window to talk to Mike. Not knowing my plans, Mom grabbed me around the waist and pulled me away. I was more frustrated than I had been in my life.

When she held me, I fought back and jabbed her with my elbow. Mom gave a surprised *ouch*, and I felt so much shame for having hurt her in my frustration. Instantly deflating, I stopped resisting, and we sat on the bed. That's when the truck started, and Mike took off, revving the engine as he went. I was sure my last chance to give him my answer had just left.

I returned to my room to find my bed sheets and blankets in a mound on the floor. Mom and Dad were standing in the doorway trying to figure out what bed to put into my room, but I asked them to leave it for the night, and they left me alone. In despair, I sat on my pathetic pile of bed sheets and blankets. What was I going to do now?

As I languished on my heap of bedding, I tried to think through my anger and defeat. After I cooled off a little and could focus again, I started to pray. I paced my room for thirty minutes, praying to God for help with my frustrations and direction on my next steps. Slowly, my mind cleared, and I calmed down. Then, as clearly as if someone had spoken to me aloud, I heard, "Tonight is the night you are leaving the Amish." My first reaction was, *How is that going to be possible? Mike has left, and I am trapped in a second-story bedroom.*

It seemed unthinkable. How was I to leave? Despite how it appeared, I believed it would happen even if I had no clue how. I realized I should prepare as much as I could for when the time came, so I got my handbag and stuffed a dress into it. I would wear my coat and shoes when I left so I was ready.

What next? By now, it was close to 10:00 p.m., which meant my siblings would be coming home from singing soon, and Mike was getting farther away.

The house was built into a hillside facing south. It had a front porch that ran the entire length of the home. The east end was where the ramp to the porch and the front door were located. My room was in the west end above the living room, where Dad and Mom sat waiting for Patrick and Melissa to get home.

Once I packed my bag, I opened my window above the porch and placed the bag on the roof outside my window. I was trying to crawl through the opening quietly, but I had one leg out when my purse started rolling away. I grabbed for it but missed. To my horror, my bag went thumping down the roof and made an audible plopping noise as it hit the half-frozen ground below.

I went back inside and sat on my pile of bedding, holding my breath, waiting for my parents to come upstairs to investigate what that thumping sound had been. After a while, when no one came, I got up and tried crawling out the window again. I made it out on the roof this time, only to find that it had started to mist sometime during the night. I stood there, trying to find a way off the roof. I considered jumping down, but I didn't want to end up breaking a leg, especially if I needed to run for it. So I just hesitated in that eerie mist on the roof with no way to retrieve my bag or get out to call Mike. Finally, I went back inside to sit on my pile of bedding again. What else was I to do?

Around 10:30 p.m., Patrick and Melissa arrived home. Patrick was asked to stay downstairs, but Melissa came upstairs with our youngest sister.

When she got to my room, she said she had news for me: "Mike is here."

I thought she had asked if he had been there, so I said, "Yes, he was here, but he left again, and I didn't even get a chance to talk to him!"

Melissa shook her head, explaining, "No, Rose, Mike is here now. We brought him back with us in the buggy. He's outside under the barn lean-to waiting to talk to you."

I could not believe my ears. "I can't get out there," I said in a hushed wail.

With a half-smile, Melissa said, "Well, Mike and I figured that might be the case, so we made a plan. You are to climb out on the roof and give Mike three flashes with a flashlight to let him know if you cannot get out of the house. You have to be careful though because Bertha and her family will be coming home from singing soon, as they attended too."

To be safe, I waited until Bertha's family arrived home, then crawled out on the roof. When I was situated, I put the light directly on me, hoping that Mike would recognize it. As I illuminated myself, I called out his name in a loud whisper.

What seemed like a long time later, he responded with, "Rose, is that you?"

"Yes! Please can you come to talk to me?"

He approached the porch and stood on the ground, gazing up at me. I was squatting on the roof, looking down at him, when Mike asked me, "Is there any way for you to get down?

"No. I tried earlier, but the only way was to jump, and I wasn't comfortable with that," I explained.

"Then, go back inside, and I'll be back at two with a ladder to get you down."

That's all we said to each other, and as I went back through the window, I felt like I was in a dream. Was this really happening?

Melissa offered for me to sleep in her room that night instead of on the pile of bedding, and I accepted her offer. I went to bed fully dressed, and as we lay there talking, I told Melissa the whole story, including the fact that I was leaving the Amish that night. It saddened Melissa, but she said she understood my decision, especially with Mike having left. "However, if you ever want to come back, please know you are always welcome."

"I'm happy to hear you say that, Melissa, but it will be for good when I leave tonight. I will never be Amish again," I pledged.

We talked for some time before I heard a faint noise. It sounded like something hitting the siding, then rolling down the porch roof and landing on the ground below with a thud. I waited in breathless silence, afraid Melissa would hear it, but she didn't mention anything as we continued talking. As I lay in Melissa's bed visiting with her, I feared Mike would be caught throwing rocks at my bedroom window. I couldn't help thinking, *Mike, I know you're out there, but I do not dare come out yet*. My family had started to settle down, but I could still hear some of my younger siblings tossing and turning in their beds, and I wasn't sure my parents were asleep yet either.

When Melissa and I were ready to say our good nights, I realized it was already one thirty. I asked Melissa to walk through the house for me on the pretense that she wanted a drink of water to see if the parents were asleep. She came back upstairs with the message that everyone was quiet and seemed to be sleeping, so we said our goodbyes. I went to my room again so Melissa could sleep before I left.

I was confident Mike was waiting for me already, so when I left Melissa's room, I headed straight for my bedroom window. I tiptoed across the hallway, barely breathing for fear that any minute someone would hear me, and I would be busted.

Once in my room, I made it to the window and opened it, crawling through it one more time. I climbed on the roof, and Mike was there with the ladder. However, I asked him to take it to the other end of the porch because my parents' bedroom on the main floor was at the same end of the house as my bedroom. I figured I would rather walk the length of the porch past Patrick and Ferman's bedrooms and risk waking them than make an unexpected noise this close to the parents' bedroom and be caught halfway down the ladder.

Mike took the ladder to the other end of the porch for me. When I finally got on the ground, I could not believe I had actually escaped. After six hours of being a prisoner in my bedroom, I was finally free. I asked Mike to meet me out on the driveway, as I had something to do first. Then, without another word, I went down the outside steps, grabbed my bag from where it had fallen earlier that night, and headed for the driveway.

When Mike saw that I had a bag, he asked, "What is that for?" He still didn't know my plans to leave with him. He thought he had helped me off that roof simply to talk to me.

Resolutely, I said, "I'm leaving the Amish tonight—if that's okay with you?"

"Are you serious? Then, let's get out of here!" Mike exclaimed, and we took off running, carrying the ladder between us. We had to walk a short distance to get to the truck, as Mike had parked it far enough away so my family would not hear it.

As we were running toward the truck, we saw headlights approaching, so we jumped into the ditch until the vehicle had passed. Then, we got up and ran some more. Fortunately, we made it to the truck without any problems. After putting the ladder in the back, we hopped into the vehicle. Then, we sat and looked at each other for a few minutes. How had we just pulled off that escape? It truly couldn't have worked out more perfectly even if we had tried to strategically plan the getaway.

With the magnitude of what we had just done restricting my lungs, I sat in the truck, telling Mike I had intended to call and ask him to pick me up a week later because I thought that would be the right time to leave the Amish. However, when I realized God's plan was for me to go that night, I said I was willing—I just didn't understand how it was possible. Ultimately, though, I realized I didn't have to understand "the how." My responsibility was to take the steps in faith. When God guided me, there would always be a way to the right thing.

CHAPTER THIRTEEN

New Beginnings

I woke up the following day at my future brother-in-law Adam's home. My thoughts went to my family, wondering what the household was like that morning. *Have they discovered that I left during the night? What are their thoughts and feelings? How bad did I hurt them?* I wished things could have been different, but I knew there was no use wishing for that, as what had happened was done. Nonetheless, I was sad knowing I would never again be part of my family. Knowing the consequences, I had made my choice, and yes, it hurt, but there was peace too.

When I went downstairs, Mike's brother and family greeted me. I had met them twice before, so we were not strangers. I'm not sure who was more surprised—Adam and Martha or their five children—to find out that Mike had arrived at night and brought his Amish girlfriend. They welcomed me into their home as part of the family, and I was extremely thankful for their generosity. From that day forward, Mike looked out for me.

At first, I thought I would keep wearing my Amish clothes. It only took two days for me to change my mind. Shopping for new clothing was a complete culture shock. It was the first time I could choose my own style. However, I still needed to decide what style I liked. In the meantime, my sisters-in-law had many friends, and it didn't take long for the news to spread that a new Amish girl was in town. The following week, clothes that people no longer needed or wanted started coming in. I rummaged through many a trash bag full of clothes to find some I could use until I could afford to buy my own. As I rummaged through the garments, I found so many styles of clothing that were considered outdated by my more sophisticated extended family. They were trying to help me find a style I liked from the options I had to choose from. However, I did not have a clue what I wanted to see on myself, so finding my own style proved to be more difficult than I thought it might be.

Another challenge was that I did not have my birth certificate or social security card. In fact, I didn't have a social security number at all. At least my birth certificate was in my birth town's courthouse. I just needed to figure out how to get it, as I didn't have any form of ID.

Seeking a solution, I called the courthouse, explained my situation, and asked how to get my birth certificate. Because I was nineteen, I was considered an adult, so if I came in, they could release it to me personally. I had to make a "loose" appointment and, when I got to the courthouse, give them my birthplace and date. Then, in return, I was provided with my birth certificate. This was the first step in gaining my independence.

Mike wanted me to get my driver's license, so he started giving me driving lessons. I was terrified the first time I sat behind the wheel, but Mike was a persistent and encouraging teacher. "You just need to practice, and you will be fine," he told me. I started practicing driving by going back and forth on Yule, another of Mike's brothers, and Elnora's long driveway, directly across the road from Abraham's. By the time I had attained my birth certificate and social security number, I was ready to take my driving test. Once I passed, I finally had my forms of ID. Another relatively small step but a monumental victory in my eyes! Next up was finding a job.

It was the middle of January when Mike, along with his brother Yule, sister Meredith, and their spouses, went to California to attend the graduation of another one of their brothers from the Marine Corps boot camp. A day after the party left for California, I was sitting in Martha's living room, reading a book to her youngest child, when Martha came running up from the basement excitedly because a minivan full of Amish people had just pulled into her driveway! I asked if it was my family, but she didn't know; she had never met my family before.

I continued reading as Martha greeted the man who stepped out of the vehicle. "Is Rosanna there?" he asked.

Martha responded, "She is. What do you want with her?"

"I want to talk to her."

103

Martha came back inside and gave me the message. With a sigh, I set my book to the side and rose from my seat. When I went out the door, I saw my dad standing beside the minivan.

"Hi, Dad," I said cautiously. "What do you want?"

"I have Mom, Patrick, and Melissa in the van, and we'd like to speak with you, but not at Abraham's home. Will you come with us to town for lunch, and we could talk while we eat?" he asked.

"I have no intention of going anywhere with you unless I have your word that you will bring me back to Martha's house when we are done," I replied firmly. Dad promised that they would return me to Martha's if that was what I wanted. "Okay. Then, I'll get my coat and be right back," I agreed.

"You must change into your Amish dress before you can ride with us," Dad warned.

After giving a stiff nod, I went back inside and told Martha the plan. However, she was unsure that I should be leaving with my parents. "What if they take you home with them?" she asked with a furrowed brow. I told her I had the same concern but explained what my dad had promised. "But do you trust him to keep his word?" she asked worriedly.

"Yes, this time, I do. They know they have no legal hold on me to take me back home again," I assured her.

Once we were all seated at FlapJacks and everyone had placed their orders, Dad opened the conversation. "Rosanna, do you realize what you are doing by leaving the

Amish church after you were baptized? Do you realize that you are damning your soul by abandoning your religion of birth for a false belief?"

"Yes, Dad, I know the Amish beliefs and understand where you are coming from, but I no longer see it your way. I feel that God led me out of the Amish for a reason I don't fully understand, but I am learning to trust and have found that having faith in where God is leading me is better than following my own direction."

Dad was not moved by my heartfelt response. In fact, he was sure it could not be God guiding me; instead, my selfish and worldly desires were leading me straight to damnation.

"I understand that is what you think, Dad, but I have no intention of ever being Amish again because I have come to realize that the Amish rules are not aligned with the Bible," I said, grasping for patience.

The one comment that stood out to me during our conversation was, "If you have made up your mind to forsake your faith, then you should know you will not live for very long."

"Are you threatening me?" I asked my dad, startled that he would say such a thing. "How else could you know I will die soon?"

Dad explained it like this: "Our family has a track record of dying soon after they leave the Amish. Therefore, you should know that your end is near if you're not coming home with us."

"Is there a reason why the death rate is so high in our family for those who leave the Amish?" I questioned, incensed by this news. In response, he said it was God's way of warning our family not to abandon their faith.

That set my mind reeling. *Why had God called me away from the Amish if it was to end my life?* Something didn't ring true to me. I needed time to pray on this matter. In the meantime, I accepted Dad's prediction for my life as he understood it, but I stood my ground on not returning home with them that day.

Later, I discovered Dad had lost a few cousins from drunk driving after they had left the Amish. That was Dad's evidence that I would meet my end as a result of leaving my community behind. In other words, God would punish me by ending my life.

Dad saw I would not change my mind, so it was time for them to go. As promised, they returned me to Martha's house and left. I was both happy and sad as they drove away—glad they had kept their promise and sad that they were going away with things being as they were between us. I wondered if we would ever have a positive relationship again. Unfortunately, it seemed unlikely.

CHAPTER FOURTEEN

Power Struggles

I had left home without any of my personal belongings. I assumed I could retrieve them after my parents knew I was no longer planning to be Amish, so a few weeks later, I returned with the intent to pick up my stuff. However, I was summarily told by my parents that I could not have them—that nothing belonged to me anymore. In their view, when I walked out the door, I forfeited all my rights to anything I had previously owned—with one exception: I could have the gifts I had received from Mike throughout our dating. They did not want anything from Mike left in their house. As for everything else, it didn't matter where it had come from or what purpose it had. It no longer belonged to me.

Frowning, I asked my parents, "To whom does it belong then?"

They replied, "Whomever we decide to give it to, just not you—unless, of course, you decide to be Amish again."

I had driven eighty miles to pick up my belongings that day just to be told I had to make an appointment to return another day for the stuff Mike had given me. I recognized this as a power move, but if I wanted my gifts from Mike, I knew I had to do as they asked. Although, I will admit, it was tempting to leave everything behind; it was just stuff anyway. I had learned that I could live with much less when it came down to it.

After this incident, I also received a hospital bill for my appendix surgery that had taken place the previous year. I was a little surprised when this happened, so I called the phone shack and left a message asking Dad to call me back. When he returned my call, I asked him why I had gotten the bill. He said, "Mom and I decided if you want to be an adult and leave home, you can start by paying your hospital bills."

"But you had been paying them before I left the Amish, and I was of age then too," I countered.

"Yes, you were nineteen, but you had been making money and working for us while living at home, so paying your bills was worth our time and money. Now that you are no longer bringing in any money or helping us out in the home, it's no longer our responsibility to pay your bill. If you want to live by Mike's family, let *them* take care of your bills," Dad declared.

Ouch! Now that hurt, but what could I say? I had chosen to leave home, and I was of age, so yes, I should pay my own bills. I had been taken to the hospital by ambulance and had yet to receive that bill, so I asked for that one as well. However, Dad responded, "It's almost paid off, so we decided to finish it."

"Well, if you're sure it's worth your money seeing as I am no longer of any benefit to you, then thank you," I said.

A few weeks later, Mike and I were running some out-of-town errands when we decided to go back to my parents' home for my things. I called the phone shack and left a message saying we were on our way and would be there later that day to pick up my stuff.

We were almost there when my dad called us back to tell me, "You have to wear your Amish clothes, or you will not be allowed to take anything with you today." This was new. Now what? We were ten minutes from their house, and I wasn't about to turn around and drive another three hours round trip just for a few dishes! Luckily, Mike had an idea. What if I asked to borrow a dress from one of his sisters? That sounded okay, so we stopped at his parents' place, and Elsie was happy to lend me a dress.

This was the second time I had seen Elsie since leaving the Amish. Although she did not approve of my decision, she was kind to me. We got to visit for a few minutes as I was getting changed into one of her dresses before we headed to my parents' house.

We arrived at my parents' home to find that we were not the only company they had. My parents had invited some couples from the church who were some of my former students' parents too. I had intended to go in, get my few boxes of dishes, then be on my way again while Mike stayed in the truck. We both knew he would not be allowed in the house anyway. Despite my best intentions, I went into the house for the first box and got stuck talking with the church members. While I was happy to speak with them, I was surprised at the nature of our conversation.

They wanted to know what my parents had done wrong to cause me to leave the Amish. While I knew some things had not been good while I was living at home, I had not left the Amish because of my parents but rather because of the church rules. My mom and dad had raised us to believe what the Amish are expected to teach their children: obey the parents and the church rules, and nothing else matters. It seemed these community members wanted me to throw my parents under the bus, but I couldn't do that. In all earnestness, I insisted they hadn't done anything "wrong" in raising me.

"Then, why have you left the Amish?" they perpetually demanded.

"Because I don't believe the church rules are enough to save me anymore."

"Do you think you are better than the rest of us?" they asked.

"No," I replied, "but I think I need to read my Bible more and find out what God wants from me. Then, I want to be faithful to that. I know I can't do that being Amish."

When I did not accuse my parents of any wrongdoing, the school parents left, and two preachers came to talk to me. They had many of the same questions. However, the tactics changed when I insisted that it wasn't anyone's fault—my decision to leave was because I wanted to live a godly life, and just being Amish wasn't cutting it. It went from, "What did your parents do wrong?" to "You are the one in the wrong. Your parents told us you were wrong, but we didn't believe them, considering how well you followed the rules after your baptism. Now, we see your parents were right."

With judgment and condemnation in their tone, they continued by saying, "This means we must put you in the baún if you are forsaking your promise to stay with the church. Do you give us the right to place the baún on you?"

"I don't believe in the baún," I said, "but you can do whatever you want. You will anyway."

Over the next thirty minutes, we went around and around about me permitting them to place the baún on me. Seeing that we were at an impasse, they finally left with, "We see now that your parents were right about you in all they said; you are a willful and disobedient child. We will have no choice but to place the baún on you if you have not returned to the Amish and confessed in two weeks."

As if I needed more validation for my recent decision to leave the Amish, I now felt more strongly that I could not agree with their belief system anymore.

Having gotten through these disruptions, I continued to my room for my first load and saw that the corner shelf Mike had given me was still on the wall. Patrick was in the room and had the screwdriver needed to take it down, so I asked him to do it for me. He said, "I will if you answer my questions first."

"Sure," I agreed. "What are they?"

"Do you think what you are doing is right?" Patrick asked.

"Yes, I think I am making the right decision for me," I answered firmly.

"Do you believe it's right for you to leave the Amish?" he continued.

"Yes, I do. Now, will you take it off the shelf?" I pressed, wanting to get in and out as swiftly as possible.

"No," he replied. "You didn't answer my questions."

"What questions did I not answer?" I asked in consternation.

To my chagrin, Patrick then asked me the same questions, and I answered them again the same way. This happened for at least ten more minutes. Every time I requested for Patrick to take down my shelf, his response was the same.

Finally, I looked at him and said, "You are not asking me because you want to know my feelings on the matter, are you? I get the feeling you want me to answer differently, but I will not give you anything but my honest opinion. You did ask me to tell the truth, after all. If you want to tell me what I'm doing is wrong, say it, but it will not change my decision."

When I ultimately asked for the screwdriver to take the shelf off myself, he said, "No, you aren't being honest and answering my questions, so you can't have the screwdriver either."

At this point, I was beyond frustrated. I realized it wasn't about answering his questions; this was just an excellent way for him to insert his power into the situation when he otherwise had none. As I stood in my mostly empty room, looking around at what had already been taken and put in storage, it again dawned on me that it was all just stuff anyway. I didn't need any of it. I just wanted out of the house and away from all the infuriating traditions and games that had been so much a part of my everyday life.

After what felt like forever, I finally returned to the truck with the first box of dishes. Before heading back into the house for another load, I sat in the truck to chat briefly with Mike, who said he had been getting worried. It had been two hours since I had gone into the house. "What is taking so long? What is happening in there?" Mike asked. I told him the situation and explained that I felt like Patrick was playing a power game with no intention to help unless he got what he wanted, which would mean I had to say I was wrong to leave the Amish. However, I refused to lie. Then, I asked for Mike's thoughts on the matter.

Mike said his dad had a star screwdriver and would probably allow us to borrow it, so we went to his parents' place. We talked with his dad for a few minutes, explaining our dilemma, and to our delight, he agreed we could borrow the tool. When we returned to my parents', I beelined into the house to take down the shelf. However, when I got there, I found it on the floor; someone must have taken it down while we were gone tracking down another screwdriver. After that, I got the rest of my stuff and went without further trouble.

On our way back to Maquoketa, Mike told me what he had experienced while waiting for me. Patrick had come up to him soon after I had gone to the house and threatened him, saying, "You are fortunate that you stayed in your truck, or I would have beaten you up. If you so much as stepped out, I had every intention of beating the crap out of you." When Mike offered to exit the vehicle and let him have a go at him, Patrick hurriedly replied, "Oh, it doesn't matter anymore because I've already told you what I would have done." Shrugging, Mike decided to leave it, as he had nothing to prove to Patrick, but clearly, Patrick needed to justify himself.

A little back story: Patrick had asked Mike to pick him up to leave the Amish on Old Christmas Day. That was the same day I had intended to leave until everything had gone down the way it had six days prior on New Year's night. I had just discovered this when Patrick called Mike to lecture him for helping me escape the Amish and then canceled his reservations for Mike to pick him up.

After that, my dad came by to chat with Mike. Dad tried to persuade him to "just leave Rosanna behind." When that failed, he tried to intimidate Mike, but he held firm, insisting, "I'm not leaving, even if it takes all night. Rose is coming with me unless she tells me herself to leave without her." After this statement, Dad exited the truck. From then on, Mike sat there undisturbed, waiting for me.

"I'm not sure what I would have done had you left without me," I said, gazing at him.

"That was never an option!" he replied vehemently.

I was overwhelmed with thankfulness for Mike's patience that day. At the same time, I was ashamed when Mike related my family's actions. I knew they blamed him for my decision to leave, but he did not deserve that treatment. In my mind, I was only getting what I deserved, but Mike was a wonderful, godly man. He only deserved the best.

CHAPTER FIFTEEN

Seeking Health

A year later, Mike and I were engaged. We planned for a small outdoor summer wedding with only close friends and family present. I did invite my family, but as expected, no one came. Even though I had not expected any of my family members to attend the wedding, it was still a disappointment when no one actually showed up.

We had decided on having the ceremony at the local state park beside a stream. There was a stone bridge that crossed the stream at one point, so we had Mike and the judge waiting on one end of the bridge while I made my way across to join them and become married to my best friend for life. With Mike's non-Amish siblings and family all present, it made for a special time despite not having any of my personal family present.

The reception was then held at the family home of a close friend. They were the ones who had given me a home before I was married, so they were very dear to me. It was a low-key wedding but just about as perfect as could be in my mind.

After we were married, we lived in an apartment in Madrid, Iowa, and life settled into a routine of work and school for me. I was in the early childhood education program and was elated that I had decided to attend college for this particular subject. I truly enjoyed working with little ones and loved the different techniques I was learning to deal with children, especially in the discipline area.

After living in Madrid for a year, we moved to Wyoming, where we resided in an apartment for another year before buying our first house. It wasn't anything fancy, but it was ours. Well, we shared it with the bank, of course!

Even though we were far from perfect, we had a happy marriage and were perfect for each other. As a married couple, we were learning how to navigate some of life's challenges. At the same time, we were trying to deal with the aftereffects of my former life. On the surface, it looked like I had everything going for me. I had a wonderful husband who loved and appreciated me. I had what I felt were genuine and sincere new friends in Wyoming. I had a good job I was passionate about. So why did I not feel peace?

The more secure my daily environment became, the more my past returned to haunt me. It was slowly spilling over the top of the walls that I had built to keep my dirty secret hidden through the years. I had reached my max in wall building and couldn't keep the horrific experiences at bay. Now what was I to do?

Always willing to turn to my life partner for support, I told Mike I was seriously struggling with my past. To put it simply, I was torn. I had a deep desire for my past to be brought to light, but at the same time, my acute shame was holding me back. For so long, I had felt that my past was a skeleton that needed to stay hidden forever lest I be seen as dirty or less of a person. Now, the impossibly heavy secret was beginning to feel like more of a burden than the fear of what people would think of me if they did find out what I'd gone through. At this point, by my knowledge, only four others knew of my past: my mom, Mike, Meredith, and my brother. (Mike had confided in his sister Meredith—with my permission—as a means to cope after learning about the abuse I endured.)

"Is it time for me to tell the rest of your family and deal with the consequences?" I asked Mike. I expected him to respond with a simple yes or no; instead, I went into a complete tailspin when he told me his family already knew. "But I never told them. How would they know? Did you tell them?" I demanded, cold with panic.

"No, I didn't tell anyone except Meredith," Mike assured me. "But my brother knows about it because he mentioned it during our recent conversation." Them being aware of my closely guarded secret was one thing, but knowing the one other person who could have told them must have done so without my permission—that was almost more than I could bear.

Aside from Mike, Meredith had become my closest friend. She was the one person who had encouraged me to trust the Holy Spirit's leadership. Meredith was the sister I had always longed to have—the one that would never turn her back on me—the one person I had thought I could trust completely. Why would she have told her family my deepest, darkest secret without telling me? Didn't she realize this would shatter the total faith I had in her trustworthiness? These and other thoughts spun relentlessly in my mind, making me dizzy.

As I struggled to accept that my extended family knew about my past without my consent, I couldn't help but ask myself this question too. *Why did I think Meredith would keep my secret to herself when I had not? Why did I expect anyone else to keep quiet if I couldn't?* I had told Mike, who had then told Meredith, who had then told her family. With this realization, I could not hold this against Meredith.

The next time I was in Iowa, I asked Meredith whether she had told the other family members about my past. When she admitted to divulging this information, I asked her why she hadn't talked to me about it first, especially after she had seen how hard it had been on me when Mike had told her. Meredith responded, "I knew it would hurt you if you found out, but I told them anyway so that they might understand you better. I hoped by the time you found out that they knew, you would be able to handle it.»

Her explanation aligned with my expectation. She had been trying to help me, not hurt me. Even though I had been deeply wounded by these actions and felt betrayed by her, once I let my emotions settle, I recognized she had not intentionally caused me pain.

While on the outside, my life looked great, on the inside, I was slowly dying. My health was deteriorating too. It reached the point that I was missing at least one day of work each week. Before long, my coworkers started asking questions about my health.

I didn't know what was wrong with me. I had been to many urgent care facilities while we lived in Iowa, and they always said nothing was wrong with me and sent me home again. It got to the point that I refused to go to a doctor at all. I knew the drill: tell them your symptoms, do a pregnancy test, answer some questions, and be sent home with the statement, "There's nothing we can do, as there's nothing wrong with you." But I *knew* there was something wrong. No ordinary person should be walking around with migraines daily, dizzy from pain and fatigue, just to be told again and again that there's nothing wrong with them. Eventually, when I consistently failed to receive the treatment I needed, I lost hope in the medical system.

Finally, a friend recommended a chiropractor to me. She warned that this particular chiropractor was "different," but maybe she could help me. Since I was frankly desperate at this point, I was willing to give her a try. After performing some tests and asking numerous questions about my health, the chiropractor told me that all my symptoms were pointing to multiple sclerosis (MS). I did not know what that was, so I asked her. Obligingly, she explained it to me, but she also encouraged me to look it up when I got home.

"If you want a diagnosis, you will need extensive testing in Mayo Clinic," she remarked.

In response, I said, "I don't care for a label; I just want to know how to cure it." Imagine my surprise when she said there is no medical cure for MS. "Then, what are my options?" I asked.

"You have a couple," she replied. "You can go the medical route, which would start with testing and diagnosis. Then, if it is MS, you can take medicine in hopes of putting the MS into remission. Or…" Abruptly, she stopped.

"Or what?" I prompted.

"Or you can go with a natural approach. Basically, you'd change your lifestyle and eating habits. Typically, if you give your body what it needs, the body will heal itself."

I closely examined my options. By my view, one offered hope, while the other one felt like a dead end. I knew I had a choice to make, and even though it sounded challenging, I determined I would go with the natural approach.

I got home from the chiropractor's office and "cleaned house." I went through my cupboards and threw out all my processed foods. The bathroom was emptied of all my cleaners with artificial smells and synthetic ingredients, and all my candles and synthetic perfumes went into the trash can. With great resolve, I stopped eating all processed sugars. The next day, I went shopping for raw, whole foods. With just a diet change and time, my health improved significantly. I could work five days a week again, and except for the occasional flare-up, the migraines disappeared too.

I was abundantly grateful to see my health starting to improve. I had always wanted to have a family someday, and it was beginning to look like that could be possible if I were committed to doing what my body needed to heal. With that in mind, I committed to learning about my body's needs. Instead of listening to others' input on what I should be doing, I listened to my body's physical response to foods and my environment. I still had a long way to go, but I was on the right track.

After seeing drastic—and positive—results from listening to my body's needs, I decided I should use the same approach toward my mental health. After all, if the natural body needs specific ingredients for optimal health, then it only makes sense that the mind needs specific "ingredients" too. But what were those specifics?

In short, I realized I had found ways to improve my natural health but lacked spiritual health. However, as I learned, mental and biological health go hand in hand with spiritual health. So that was where I needed to start.

CHAPTER SIXTEEN

The Walls Break

While trying to get a grip on my natural health, I realized my emotional health needed some healing too. The time had come for me to allow my past to be my past, but how? I had been praying for years that I could forgive my brother and never talk about it again, so why did it keep coming up when I least expected it? Shouldn't I be able to forget about it if I had forgiven him? I had been taught to forgive someone meant I'd never talk about the offense again. So why was I feeling pushed to talk about it more instead of less? Had I not forgiven my brother after all? What was wrong with me? How did I expect forgiveness to be extended if I couldn't forgive him and others? Simply put, I was an emotional mess.

I knew I had to talk with Wilbur about what had happened and see if he had changed. Maybe he had and would recognize how wrong his actions had been. With this hope hot in my chest, I went to see Wilbur the next time we were in Iowa. He was working in his furniture shop when I arrived.

"What are you doing here?" he asked in surprise when I walked in.

Holding firm in my desire to achieve spiritual freedom, I blurted out an emotional response. "I want to know why you did to me what you did in the past. Did I do something wrong that you decided was worthy of punishment? Was there something wrong with me? Was it because I was not as pretty as my sisters? Why, Wilbur? Why?"

"No," said Wilbur. "It was none of that."

"Then, why?" I demanded.

"Because we liked it. It felt good—that's why we did it. I did it with you because you were special to me," Wilbur explained.

"Is it okay to hurt someone else for your pleasure because you think they are special?" I asked. "Do you seriously think I liked it? Why do you think I was always fighting you and trying to run away if it had been 'fun' for me? And did you ever use protection?"

"No," Wilbur admitted.

"Did it ever cross your mind that I could have gotten pregnant?"

"Yes, it did. I guess God was looking out for us." Wilbur shrugged.

I was speechless! I could not wrap my head around that statement. Did he really say what I thought I had heard him say? I could not believe my ears!

Yes, I believed with all my heart that God had protected me, but it simply did not sit well with me that Wilbur would credit God's protection as if he had not deliberately chosen to abuse me, then turn around and proclaim God's greatness. It may have been "small" of me to think that, but this was more confirmation that Wilbur's actions spoke louder than his words. Although his words included God's name, they were empty to me. With nothing further to say to the man who had tortured me growing up, I turned and walked back to the car where Mike awaited me.

When I returned to the vehicle and collapsed into my seat, I told Mike it was hopeless. Wilbur admitted that something had happened—because "WE" liked it. I had seen no remorse and had heard no regret coming from him. Wilbur had not acknowledged that his behavior had been wrong and should not have happened.

Seeing my devastation and defeat, Mike encouraged me to seek counseling, but I refused. Having been through mandatory abuse training in my line of work with children, I knew what was bound to happen if I got counseling. I did not want to be the cause of my brother possibly going to jail.

We went home, and I tried to continue my life, but things weren't progressing positively. I started having nightmares more frequently. I would wake up in cold sweats because of the visions in my dreams—Wilbur using his daughter the way he had used me with no one there to help her. When these nightmares continued to plague me, they put things into a different perspective. I was no longer quite as determined to deal with my past my way. I felt no need to report Wilbur for what he had done to me. What would be the point? It could not change the past anyway. However, I did not want to be an enabler or accomplice to him either! I couldn't stand the thought of him possibly abusing other girls. Even though I was sure he had also abused some of my younger sisters, having the nightmares of him abusing my niece really kicked things into a different perspective. I didn't know what to do.

Six months later, I was finally willing to seek counseling, but I wanted to talk with my brother one more time beforehand. I figured if he had repented, I would not need counseling. In my mind, that would mean my fears were just that—baseless fears—and would render my nightmares invalid. Mike agreed to go with me to visit Wilbur and be present for the conversation on one condition: I had to consent to see a psychologist after the visit if things did not change. Ultimately, I conceded. I was desperate for peace and had exhausted all my other resources with no positive results. This visit was my last desperate effort in hopes that things could be settled peacefully.

We headed to Iowa that summer. This time, I called ahead and asked Wilbur's neighbor to tell him that I was coming to Iowa to talk with him and even gave the specific date. His neighbor agreed to pass along the message.

When that day came, we arrived at Wilbur's place to find him gone. I asked Malinda about it, and she admitted the neighbor had brought the message. Still, Wilbur had decided not to concern himself over the announcement, as he was sure the topic I wanted to discuss was unimportant anyway. So he had left for the afternoon.

"Do you know when he is coming home?" I had no doubt that Wilbur had deliberately chosen not to be home that day, but it didn't surprise me. Determined to have the conversation we had come there for, Mike and I decided to wait for him to return home. We had come this far and had no intention of leaving again without talking with Wilbur as a couple this time.

Mike and I waited outside the rest of the afternoon until Wilbur finally arrived. He didn't look happy to see me. My suspicions were confirmed when I walked up to him and received a "What in the world are you doing here again?" As if he didn't know we were coming.

"I need to talk to you," I insisted.

"If it's about the past, we have already talked about that, and it's time to let it go," Wilbur said.

"I know we have talked once, but we need to talk again. Mike will be present this time," I pressed.

Wilbur brushed me off and returned to his neighbor and driver. I knew the driver, so I went over and said hi to him before leaving him and Wilbur alone to visit some more. After the neighbor left, Wilbur headed to the furniture shop, and Mike and I followed him.

Malinda joined us right away too. Ever the loyal wife, she asked me why I was bringing up things that had already been taken care of. In her view, it should now be forgiven and not brought up again.

At this point, I lost all diplomacy and patience. I led with my raw and humiliated emotions. I felt like I was in the wrong for wanting to deal with my past instead of continuing to ignore it, so I did not stop to think about the other players in the shop that night, nor did I mince my words. I simply blurted out, "Did you know Wilbur raped me while I lived at home? Did he tell you that was what I had come to talk to him about a year ago? If he did, then you are as bad as he is."

After my outpouring of emotion, there was silence all around, and the children were told to leave the shop. I didn't care that my outburst had shocked everyone; I was on a mission. I thought I knew the answer, but I needed to know with certainty whether Wilbur had molested my sisters and if he regretted that. Wilbur finally admitted that he had touched them but had never gone as far with any of them as he had with me. This did not comfort me but rather confirmed my suspicions and fears. I was adamant that what he had done was wrong! It did not matter who did it or whom it had happened to—it was wrong, and there could be some seriously long-lasting consequences for both parties depending on how things were handled.

"We have talked about this already; it's unnecessary to discuss it again. Why can you not forgive and move on with your life?" Wilbur wanted to know.

Mike tried talking to Wilbur, attempting to help my brother see how the horrors of my past at his hands was affecting my life in negative ways. He said that he was encouraging me to speak to a psychologist, but I first needed to know if there was any regret in Wilbur.

"Why would she have to speak to a psychologist for help?" Wilbur asked with utmost ignorance.

This comment was the straw that broke the camel's back. Dumbstruck by Wilbur's blasé attitude, I could not speak anymore. I stood silently sobbing, tears streaming down my cheeks. My mind was blown! How could Wilbur not see what he had done was wrong, then repent and ask forgiveness? I knew my time for talking with Wilbur was over. What was the point?

Without another word, I left the group and went to sit outside the shop, desperately grappling with my emotions. The other adults stayed inside talking for a bit longer, leaving me to work through my bitter feelings on my own.

As I sat outside the shop door, it was only a short time before I had company. My two young nephews and niece joined me. Seeing their sweet, innocent faces helped me find some semblance of calm. We started talking and playing around, and it hit me with a fresh burst of pain. What if I was too late to help my niece? Was she in harm's way because of me?

On the one hand, I felt very selfish, but on the other hand, I felt helpless! If I reported my brother, I would send these innocent little children's dad to prison. But would he mistreat them too if I *didn't* report him? I was now convinced that Wilbur had no regrets about the past, but would he go so far as to molest his own daughter? Clearly, he did not see what he had done as being bad. It was simply a way to have fun, and the person he was "having fun with" in the past had made no difference to him. Why did I think it would make a difference now?

I had gone through something horrible; others might have to live that nightmare too if I was too selfish and weak to admit that my brother was an abuser. If that happened, I knew I would be partly to blame. Until now, I had refused to make a stand out of fear and shame for myself. Now, it was time for that to change. I was ready to move out of denial and embrace the consequences that were sure to follow.

I played with the children until Mike exited the shop and said he was ready to go. My heart was unbearably heavy when we left that night. On the way home, I asked Mike, "Was there any remorse Wilbur showed that I wasn't able to recognize because of my emotions?"

Mike confirmed that my raw emotions did not change the facts—he had not heard remorse from Wilbur either. It did not seem as if Wilbur understood that he had actually done anything wrong. His careless language made it seem like it wasn't a big deal that he'd molested his sisters. By his skewed reasoning, it had all been done in fun, nothing else. Hearing Mike's confirmation was sickening and liberating to me.

Once we got home, I earnestly began my search for a psychologist. That was the deal, but regardless, I now couldn't deny I needed some outside help. After calling around, I found Lucy, a fantastic psychologist whom I started seeing once a week during my lunch break. Although I tried to mentally prepare myself for psychological release, I had no idea the floodgates were about to be opened. I was so focused on finding out the chances of repentance for a pedophile that it took a few sessions for me to stop trying to justify my brother and ask for help for myself.

Although I was the one who had booked my sessions to talk to Lucy about my past, it took some time before I was able to tell her what had happened. When Lucy found out, she told me that as a psychologist, she would have to report my brother, not for what he might do but because of what he had already done.

Lucy offered me the right to be silent, assuring me she would take care of everything while I stood behind her. This was new—having someone who had no attachment to me whatsoever offer to fight for me while I remained sheltered. I wanted to simply hide that way, but I felt it would not be very honorable to do so.

I left Lucy's office in despair. What was the right choice? Could I allow her to do what I saw as my dirty work? How could I report my own brother? Wasn't that sinful of me? If I allowed Lucy to report him, I could say it wasn't my doing— my hands "were tied." But were they really?

No, I realized I had a choice to make, and no matter how reticent I was to take action, I would make the right decision. I could no longer bear the thought that if I weren't willing to report my brother, I would be an accomplice to his actions. I would be helping him hurt others instead of protecting them.

Despite my conviction, I wrestled with the options set before me. *Do I report my brother and press charges or not? What will my family think of me then? They already don't like me, but this will make them hate me.*

I was right back to where I had been at thirteen years old, when I had desperately asked for God's guidance and been prompted to talk to my English neighbor. At that time, I had rejected the prompting because I had feared what it would do to my family, feeling it would be my fault if the family structure were torn apart. Now, as an adult, a few things had changed, but the same answer was before me, given straight from God. This time, I had supporters and understood that I was in this impossible situation because of Wilbur's choices. But that did not matter. What mattered was my choice, not how I'd come to the point that I needed to make it.

I didn't understand how God's answer compelled me to report my brother. Why would He have given me a family if I was not to protect and love them? I was so miserable and desperately wanted some other path to follow. The tears I cried and the overwhelming pity I felt for myself were not pretty. I just wanted peace in my life but not at this terrible cost!

While struggling to accept the choices set before me and find another answer, the thought of suicide came unbidden to my mind. Until then, I had not considered that avenue. But why not? That would take care of everything. I would not have to report my brother, and my family wouldn't hate me. Even if they did, I would never know it. And I wouldn't have to deal with my past anymore; I could end it all with me. The more I entertained the thought of suicide, the more appealing it became.

I had heard of people committing suicide, and I had thought it was a terrible thing. How could someone take their own life? Did they not realize that didn't fix anything? As I sat thinking about the suicides I had heard about, I remembered what my friend had said during a conversation about someone's decision to end their life. She commented that suicide is the coward's way out and fixes nothing.

When I remembered this conversation, my eyes were opened, and the horror of what I had been contemplating hit me. Contempt for myself hit fast and hard. I wondered what had made me go down that path anyway. Was I so desperate to avoid reporting my brother that I was willing to take my own life? There was only one thing left to do, and I hit my knees in humble submission, pleading for forgiveness.

The love I felt coming from the Holy Spirit was overpowering. I was reminded there on my knees that Jesus had already forgiven me—I just needed to accept it. I felt like I didn't deserve His forgiveness; I was so unworthy of His grace and mercy, but I was reminded again that although I can never be worthy of Jesus's forgiveness and love, it was offered anyway. The least I could do was accept it and allow His love to become my guide in life, thus bringing glory to my Heavenly Father.

These and many other Bible verses comforted me during those days: Matthew 11:28-30, "*Come to me, all you who are weary and burdened, and I will give you rest. Take my yoke upon you and learn from me, for I am gentle and humble in heart, and you will find rest for your souls. For my yoke is easy, and my burden is light.*"

How could I deny my Savior anything when He had already died for me and promised rest for my soul? This is what I had been praying for: rest for my soul. It was time to either accept God's will and love for my life or take my own way. After this loving reminder, my choice was made to surrender completely.

I decided I would rather obey God, even if that meant being hated by others, than be judged by God and found lacking. I realized that if I wanted God's blessings, I would have to do what He asked me to do. Even though I had ignored Him for many years, when I wanted my past to be forgiven, I was asked to do the same thing God had asked me to do from the beginning. My worldly concerns remained, but with my heart held lovingly in God's gentle hands, I forged ahead on the path He had set for me.

CHAPTER SEVENTEEN

Legal Proceedings

*I*n the end, I told Lucy I was ready to report my brother, and I would press charges. I could not hide behind her, but I said I would love for her to walk alongside me. To my great relief and gratitude, Lucy was beside me all the way.

Together, we called the Iowa police department, and things rapidly started happening in the legal system. At this point, I told my boss, Kari, about the situation. I had to take some phone calls during work hours and knew I would possibly need time off for some of the legal proceedings that were bound to occur. Kari was very supportive and asked me to keep her informed.

I didn't know how things would turn out, but I no longer worried about how I might look to others. One daily goal was to submit to my Savior and allow the Holy Spirit to guide me. The only real thing to me was that without Christ, I would be lost for all eternity. I could not see beyond this stage, but I had faith and hope in the one I had given my complete trust to.

During this time of trial, I sat beside mountain streams as often as possible. The sound of the rushing water and the trees all around me made God's presence very real to me. If it had been possible, I would have stayed there all day, every day, and even now, when I'm grappling with life's choices, I long to sit beside a rushing mountain stream. If that's impossible, I can at least get into nature and allow God's creation to remind me of His love.

Sara, the lawyer handling my case, had been brought in by the district attorney because she specialized in these types of cases. When she contacted me, she explained her role and laid out what would be expected from me. I was told we would probably go to court that summer if Wilbur and his lawyer didn't make a plea bargain.

Of course, I was praying it would not go to court so I wouldn't have to relive the horror Wilbur had put me through, but the district attorney and officers on my case were hoping for a court session. They indicated they were positive molestation happened far more often than reported among the Amish, and they desperately wanted people to start reporting the abusive behavior. Hopefully, if one person—me—came forward, others would as well when they saw the support from law enforcement.

In May, Mike and I took off work to go to Iowa for the initial legal proceedings, my deposition with Wilbur and his lawyer. My understanding was that a deposition was to give Wilbur's lawyer a chance to question me about the abuse and find out what he was up against. I thought it was to help them decide if they wanted to make a plea bargain. I expected questions concerning the statement that I had given to the authorities with my initial report. With this in mind, imagine my surprise when most of the questions were based on my involvement with my two younger brothers leaving the Amish the past year. The details the lawyer had and the questions he asked completely took me by surprise. However, I had no problem talking about how I had helped my brothers and what I had encouraged them to do. I was happy to talk about anything other than the hurt Wilbur had inflicted on me.

To give you a bit of context, my two younger brothers had left the Amish after me. Ferman went first. I gave him a home for a while until he got on his feet with a job and such. Then, a few years later, when my youngest brother, Daniel, wanted to leave, he asked for my help. I told him I was willing to assist, but he would have to find his own transportation to my house, as I had no intention of going to pick him up and bring him home. That would have required me to take a minor across state lines, and I knew that was not something I was willing to risk. But if he found a different means of transportation, my parents would not be as likely to press charges.

In the end, Ferman and Daniel made their own choices, and I respected the path they struck out on, just as I understood and respected my family and friends who chose to commit their lives to the Amish church and lifestyle. I was always happy to support my loved ones doing what they deemed best for them—even if my family looked poorly upon me supporting Ferman and Daniel once they left the Amish.

Incidentally, after a few years of exploring, going back and forth between being Amish and non-Amish, Daniel met a girl among the Amish he wanted to date. In the end, he decided to rejoin the Amish and marry that girl.

As we started our deposition, it felt like we were just having an everyday kind of conversation. I didn't feel uneasy in the least. Even though I was surprised at some of the information the lawyer had concerning my brothers leaving the Amish, I willingly gave more details than what the lawyer had if I felt like he didn't have the full report, so to speak, on my involvement with the boys leaving. It never crossed my mind to give anything less than full honesty.

Just before the meeting was completed, I was asked how accurate my statement of my brother Wilbur's actions was. Would I declare in a court of law that they were true? Although I became very emotional, I said 100 percent. While I could not change what had been done, I was no longer afraid to admit what had transpired either.

At this point, the lawyer asked me if I realized that my course of action was determining my brother's future—that I was the only one who could change the outcome for him. If I chose not to remove my charges against him, he would likely end up in jail. "Is that what you want for your brother?" he demanded.

Sara immediately came to my defense. She was extremely upset with the lawyer for placing the blame on me and insisted that I did not have to respond to that comment. I was touched by Sara's defense of me, but I asked permission from her to answer him anyway.

With her permission, I emotionally responded, "Yes, this is a hard truth I have already accepted; otherwise, I would not be in this office today. I have accepted that because of Wilbur's past actions, I am being forced to make some hard decisions, and with lots of prayer, I have come to this answer. It is time to turn everything over to the law and allow them to handle it according to the legal system. I have no desire to see Wilbur in jail, but if that is the outcome, I trust that is what needs to happen."

After the questionnaire, Sara and I discussed my responses, and during that conversation, I mentioned that the questions I had been asked were strange to me. At that point, Sara told me that their strategy was to prove me a liar.

"How could that work out when the officers already have Wilbur on record stating that he molested me?" I asked in surprise.

"That's a good point," she conceded. "It won't hold up in court, but so far, your family has been adamant that you are a liar and, therefore, not to be believed."

We returned home, waiting to hear back from the other party. Would Wilbur take a plea bargain? The waiting was unbearably difficult, but a few weeks later, my prayers were answered—Wilbur agreed to a plea deal. From there, the court date for sentencing was set. Sara wanted me to be in Iowa in case something changed and they backed out of the plea deal last minute. In that case, I needed to be available to go to court immediately. Sara didn't want to give them any reason to try to push back the court dates. For one thing, I was seven months pregnant when we planned to be in court, and if it got pushed back much longer, we would have to wait until after the baby was born. Nobody wanted that. So a month later, we were back in Iowa.

As we prepared for the sentencing in court, Sara told me it was typical for the judge to ask me if I wanted to give a statement in court toward the end of the session. With firm resolve, I said I would accept. Sara encouraged me to write down my message so I had something to reference once I got to the witness stand. So I grabbed a paper and pen and settled into my seat. Then, taking a deep breath with a blank page before me, I began praying for words to speak—words of truth that I could speak in love.

I tried to write them down so I could just read them, but every time I attempted to create my message, my mind wiped completely clean. I could not think of anything I wanted to say. Instead of words to write, the words of Mark 13:11 kept coming to me. "But when they shall lead *you*, and deliver you up, take no thought beforehand what ye shall speak, neither do ye premeditate: but whatsoever shall be given thee in that hour, that speak ye: for it is not ye that speak, but the Holy Ghost."

Although I wasn't being brought before the judge because I stood for Christ, I knew I had to trust the Holy Spirit to give me the words to proclaim once I was before my family, my friends, and the judge. I prayed for faith and a willingness to submit to God's will so the Holy Spirit could speak through me—and that it would not just be me lashing out in revenge against my brother and family. Finally, on the morning of the sentencing, I accepted this and said, "Okay, Lord, I will trust you to give me the words I am to speak." I never wrote a single word of my statement in court that day. I never needed to.

Toward the end of the session, I was permitted to give my statement. As I sat up in front of everyone else and beside the judge, I looked out over the crowd to find it was full. My Amish family and former friends were off to one side behind Wilbur and his lawyer. On the other side, behind Mike and my lawyer, were my extended family and friends. It hit me then that no blood family stood with me.

I was tempted to be sorry for myself for a few minutes, but I was reminded that blood family wasn't the most important thing. Instead of looking at what I did not have, I looked at what I *did* have. I had peace despite what was happening at that moment in time. In addition, I realized that most of the people in attendance had no idea about the battle that had been fought or the victory that had been given through the Holy Spirit when I had submitted to the Lord.

However, one person who had recognized and commented on my peace and calm as we prepared to go to court was in attendance: my sister-in-law Meredith. She had talked to me about it the day before, and I had told her it was not me but Christ in me that produced that peace. To this day, I know that if there is any good in me, it is because of Christ within. On my own, I would not have been able to find true peace.

After giving my statement, I realized I had just said goodbye to my family. A door was now closed. No matter how sad I was, there was nothing I could do at this time to open that door again.

In my statement I focused on what family should look like. I explained that my father should have been willing to stand and protect his daughter. I stated that a brother should be a protector to his sister, not someone his own sister should need protection from. That was just messed up.

Yes, at first, I had been bitter toward them for having failed me so miserably, but with time, I had accepted God's grace for myself, and with that, I could freely forgive them too, although I had no blood family who supported me. If they elected to stand with someone who chose to molest another person in fun and they could not see the wrong in that, I was willing to say goodbye. I had a family in Christ who would be mine for all eternity. I stood before them that day without any revenge in my heart toward them, and I prayed that God would be able to show them the same love He had shown me and thus bring freedom and forgiveness to them too.

With an open heart and the strength granted by Christ, I turned and faced the unknown, sure of only one thing:

no matter where the path led me, I wanted to stay in God's will. As I obey God's leading, there is more peace and hope in the "unknown" than what the known could ever offer without God.

I have come to understand there is but one thing that can overcome everything—one thing that will stand the test of time and continue throughout all eternity. That is the love of Christ. When I am submitted to Him, love prevails!

Epilogue

Years have passed since I went to court with my brother. As I'm sure you can imagine, I do not have a great relationship with most of my family, but I am thankful·for the few family members I do remain connected with. Part of the reason I do not maintain ties with my immediate family is the fact that I have left the Amish church. When religion is the strongest thing we have, we are bound to follow that religion. With that in mind, I do not fault my family or anyone else for following what they believe in, for this is something we all do. However, since I have tasted of God's amazing grace, I want to allow the Holy Spirit to examine me daily and show me how to live in His grace towards those I come in contact with throughout the day.

Over the years, I have learned many lessons. One of the most important lessons was how to apply the choice I made during that court experience—to live for Christ unashamed. During some of the harder lessons, I had the privilege of learning the meaning of these verses in Matthew 22:37-40:

"Love the Lord your God with all your heart and with all your soul and with all your mind." This is the first and greatest commandment. And the second is similar: *"Love your neighbor as yourself."* All the laws and prophets hang on these two commandments.

Upon reflection, I realized this means I must show love to others regardless of what I receive in return. It does not matter what someone else gives to me but rather what I give back to them. If I want man's approval, I will seek what the group or individual I'm trying to please requires, but if I want God's peace, I need to seek His approval. I am thankful I have learned this, and when I struggle with any particular issue, I am reminded to check whose requirements I should be seeking and then to choose accordingly.

We all have the right to choose our own pathway. May we be reminded we do not have to walk the path alone. With God beside us and within us, we can tread the path from darkness to light in love and peace forever. In closing, this is my prayer for all of us: that the God of love, mercy, forgiveness, and peace be with us as we walk this journey called life!

Acknowledgments

To my husband, who walked beside me whenever possible through all my highs and every low. You never gave up on me but encouraged me from day one to embrace the truth head on and not be fearful of the storm. You lovingly pushed me to write this book long before I had the vision or courage to share my story. Thank you for being you. Your patience and continued support throughout this journey have helped me stay focused and reassured.

Thank you to Megan Mohlis for being my friend and encouraging me to be true to my core beliefs. You helped me see good in myself when others were desperately trying to show me there was no good left. Yes, I give full credit for that good to Christ within, but I am thankful for your support in helping me keep believing in that power.

Thank you, Rachelle Castor, for being my "mother, big sister, and friend" all wrapped up in one beautiful person. I appreciate you reading multiple copies of my book and continuing to show love and support in so many areas of my life. Thanks also for your advice while I was navigating the unknown waters of the printing world.

Thank you, Karen Shriver, for inspiring me to share the hope I hold within with others and for helping me find the courage to continue writing.

Thank you, Lauren Green, my editor-in-chief, who heard my desire to not only share my story but to do so in love. With that in mind, your suggestions had a deep and meaningful effect. I never once in any of your suggested edits felt like you were trying to change my story or put your own spin on it. You understood my desire to show love while being completely honest despite the circumstances and thus encouraged me to make it as authentic as possible.

Thank you, Kayleigh Rucinski (and Lauren), for working with me on the book cover. I will always appreciate your willingness to try to incorporate my ideas, and when those fell to pieces due to unfortunate circumstances at the last hour, you listened to my concerns and helped me figure out a way forward.

Thank you to the complete team at Ballast Books, who worked hard with and for me to help make my publishing journey the best in every possible way.

Thank you to my friends who have been a constant source of inspiration in my life due to the love they have for Christ in their own lives.

To all of you—you know who you are—who prompted me "to write a book" after hearing a little bit of my journey. Even though I do not remember all of your names, I remember your message. Thank you for the encouragement. Although it may have taken ten to fifteen years for me to listen to your advice, here we are today. Never underestimate the power of planting a good seed, for we never know when the time will be right for it to take root and grow into something beautiful.